DEPARTMENT OF THE NAVY
HEADQUARTERS UNITED STATES MARINE CORPS
WASHINGTON, DC 20380-0001

MCO P11240.106B
LFS-2
5 Jan 00

<u>MARINE CORPS ORDER P11240.106B</u>

From: Commandant of the Marine Corps
To: Distribution List

Subj: GARRISON MOBILE EQUIPMENT

Encl: (1) LOCATOR SHEET

Reports Required:
    I. Local Procurement Status Report (Report Control Symbol EXEMPT), par. 3003
    II. Long-Term Lease Report (Report Control Symbol DN-11240-01), par. 4005
    III. Agency Report of Motor Vehicle Data (Report Control Symbol DD-11240-01), par. 8006

1. <u>Purpose</u>. To publish policy and procedures for garrison mobile equipment (GME) issued by the Commandant of the Marine Corps (CMC). This Manual provides administrative and technical instructions, policies, and procedures for all personnel involved in the management of procurement, operation, and maintenance of GME.

2. <u>Cancellation</u>. MCO P11240.106A.

3. <u>Summary of Revisions</u>. This Manual has been reformatted and contains major changes. The major changes are as follows:

    a. <u>Paragraph 2006.3.</u> Updated to conform to current Department of Defense (DoD) policy with regard to providing transportation support for morale, welfare, and recreation support services.

    b. <u>Paragraph 2011.3.</u> Includes more stringent policy for vehicle usage rates.

    c. <u>Paragraph 2012</u>. Licensing, includes more stringent policy with regard to administrative use, automotive equipment, and references the source of engineer equipment licensing procedures.

DISTRIBUTION STATEMENT A: Approved for public release; distribution is unlimited.

d. Paragraph 7007. Updated to provide specific supply support policy for GME maintenance.

e. Table 8-1. Contains updated GME Codes and additional Manufacturer Codes.

f. Added chapter 9. Inspection, Testing, and Certification of Load Lifting Equipment.

4. Responsibilities

a. The Deputy Chief of Staff for Installations and Logistics (DC/S I&L), under the direction of the CMC, has managerial responsibility for the functional areas of GME. The DC/S I&L exercises responsibility through central inventory management including planning and programming, guidance, budgeting, initial acquisition, and replacement of equipment, accounting for the total inventory, and approving and monitoring equipment allowances.

b. Commanders, including installation or activity commanders, commanding officers, inspector-instructors, or district directors, are responsible for all GME assigned to them.

c. Commanders will assign a single GME fleet manager for the operation and maintenance of GME. The GME fleet manager is the only person authorized to acquire GME for that installation. It is incumbent upon all personnel exercising supervisory responsibility to prevent abuse or misuse of equipment as well as to promote its safe operation, proper care, and productive use.

d. Operators assume direct responsibility for equipment assigned or dispatched to them. This responsibility includes safe operation, proper use, performance of such periodic maintenance as may be prescribed, and collection of operational data as may be required.

5. Recommendations. Submit recommendations concerning the contents of this Manual to the CMC (LFS-2) via the appropriate chain of command.

6. Reserve Applicability. This Manual is applicable to the Marine Corps Reserve.

7. Certification. Reviewed and approved this date.

                        G. S. McKISSOCK
                        Deputy Chief of Staff for
                        Installations and Logistics

DISTRIBUTION: PCN 10211764600

     Copy to: 7000110 (55)
               8145001 (1)
               8145004,005/7000093 (2)
               7000144 (1)

3

LOCATOR SHEET

Subj: GARRISON MOBILE EQUIPMENT

Location: (Indicate the location(s) of the copy(ies) of this
          Manual.)

ENCLOSURE (1)

GARRISON MOBILE EQUIPMENT

RECORD OF CHANGES

Log completed change action as indicated.

Change Number	Date of Change	Date Entered	Signature of Person Incorporating Change

i

GARRISON MOBILE EQUIPMENT

CONTENTS

GARRISON MOBILE EQUIPMENT

CHAPTER 1

INTRODUCTION

GARRISON MOBILE EQUIPMENT

CHAPTER 1

INTRODUCTION

1000. **DEFINITION.** GME consists of commercially available owned, leased, or otherwise controlled passenger vehicles, cargo vehicles, material handling equipment, engineer equipment, and railway rolling stock. GME fleet managers operate their GME fleets in support of transportation and maintenance requirements at Marine Corps activities. They will not use their GME fleet for tactical purposes, nor will they deploy GME assets.

1001. **GENERAL INFORMATION**

1. Effective control over the operation and use of GME requires close attention to the organization and management of resources. The goal of GME fleet managers is to provide optimum efficiency, responsiveness, effectiveness, and support of military missions, while maintaining economy of resources.

2. GME fleet managers will use GME fleet assets to the fullest possible extent to meet general support requirements so as to reduce usage and preserve readiness of tactical equipment.

3. The basic policy governing operational management of all items of GME is to provide maximum mission-essential service with the minimum equipment fleet. GME fleet managers will meet this objective by adhering to the equipment operational requirements outlined in this Manual, continually evaluating their equipment assignment methods including item-to-task suitability, and analyzing actual equipment usage.

4. TM 4700-15/1 contains instructions for completion and use of GME related forms. However, the CMC (LFS-2) authorizes and encourages the use of any locally produced or electronic forms and reports that convey the same level of information. GME fleet managers should coordinate the use of electronic forms and reports with the CMC (LFS-2) prior to use or submission.

1002. **RESOURCES MANAGEMENT**

1. The single most important factor in the effectiveness of the GME program is the involvement of the installation commander and the GME fleet manager in the management of GME resources and operations. Activity commanders, considering factors of

missions, geographic layout, location of installations and facilities, types of equipment assigned, and the requirements of this Manual, will establish standard operating procedures (SOP) for their GME fleet. The following are some of the essential procedures for effective operation and resource management:

   a. Provide maximum pooling of all equipment.

   b. Establish procedures for assignment and use of equipment.

   c. Establish central dispatch points for control.

   d. Maintain flexibility to meet changing requirements.

   e. Provide for the most economical use of manpower and equipment.

   f. Provide for training of personnel.

   g. Ensure the safety, security, and proper use of equipment.

   h. Where practical, provide for rotation of equipment among using organizations to equalize use.

   i. Provide for collection of operational and cost data as a basis for inventory and allowance actions, and performance or cost evaluation and reporting.

   j. Maintain focus on proper operator's maintenance.

   k. Maintain allowances and sub-allowances.

   l. Ensure expeditious performance of scheduled and corrective maintenance.

2. In determining the appropriate use of equipment resources, GME fleet managers must also consider the following:

   a. Each person is responsible for exercising thrift in the expenditure of public resources. Thus, where other means of service support are reasonably available, management discretion should preclude furnishing Government-owned equipment for services that are not essential.

   b. The possible liability incurred as a result of personal injury, loss, or damage of property when authorizing requests for transportation of civic groups, religious organizations, scout activities, etc.

GARRISON MOBILE EQUIPMENT

CHAPTER 2

OPERATIONS

TABLE

CHAPTER 2

OPERATIONS

2000. POOLING

1. The physical and administrative pooling of equipment to the maximum extent possible will eliminate duplication of effort, facilities, and services. However, mission, distance, economy, effectiveness, emergency functions, or other factors may indicate sub-pools to be the most practical method of operation. Any equipment sub-pools will remain under the control of the GME fleet manager.

2. GME fleet managers will use automotive equipment on a pooled basis to help ensure the highest effective level of utilization and will not assign assets exclusively to any one official or employee.

3. Users will not park or garage GME outside the confines of the installation where assigned and will not be parked in quarters' areas or at the domicile of the user. To improve security, all GME aboard installations will be parked within a motor pool when not being used over night. In instances where GME fleet managers authorize the parking or garaging of vehicles in areas away from the parent installation, vehicle operators will make every effort to use parking facilities of other military installations or the nearest State or local Government property wherever practical. Where such facilities are not available, GME fleet managers may authorize operators to use commercial parking facilities that provide for the safety and security of the equipment.

2001. DISPATCHING AND OPERATORS

1. General Information. GME fleet managers will determine the most suitable system for control of equipment and collection of pertinent data. GME fleet managers may use automated or manual systems utilizing either standard or locally generated forms. However, the system employed will be compatible with Headquarters Marine Corps (HQMC) reporting requirements. When using DD, NAVMC, or SF forms, prepare them per TM 4700-15/1.

2. While GME fleet managers may record additional data as determined by local requirements, any system utilized will include the following elements:

   a. Fuel control, including type and quantity of fuel used by each vehicle.

    b. Miles or hours of operation.

    c. Operator qualification and assignment.

    d. Operator maintenance checks and services.

    e. Report of need for corrective maintenance.

    f. Personnel and cargo statistics.

3. Active duty personnel will wear the appropriate military uniform when operating government vehicles. Under unusual circumstances, installation commanders may authorize the wearing of appropriate civilian attire if such attire is better suited to the mission.

4. Officers Driving. Officers will not drive a government vehicle (commercial or tactical) except for those selected billets which may require an officer to drive. In those instances where a determination is made that an officer is required to operate a government vehicle, the officer will obtain authorization from the installation commander or district director. Both the GME fleet manager and the officer will maintain a copy of the authorization for its duration.

5. Operation of GME by Key Volunteers. Key Volunteers shall not operate GME, but are authorized transportation as passengers when in the execution of their volunteer duties.

2002. ASSIGNMENT CLASSIFICATIONS

1. General Information. Subsequent to pooling resources and the establishment of administrative control under dispatching authority, GME fleet managers will screen mission requirements against equipment resources. Normally, such evaluation will indicate that short term dispatching of equipment (including "taxi" vehicles or equipment operated by users) will meet the majority of the installation's requirements. GME fleet managers will not exclusively assign GME to a single official or employee unless required by the nature of their responsibilities, frequency, extent, or urgency of their requirements for the equipment. Justifiable requirements and the categories described in the following paragraphs will assist in determining proper assignment for all types of equipment.

2. Class A. This class applies to automotive equipment and authorizes a continuing assignment of one of two types. Personnel authorized class A assigned vehicles will use such vehicles for official duties only, and will not reassign such vehicles to others not entitled to class A assignments.

a. The two types of class A assignments are as follows:

(1) Continuing assignment of passenger carrying vehicles to those command positions authorized full-time assignment by law and as approved by the Secretary of Defense. This authorization is for the CMC.

(2) Continuing assignment of passenger carrying vehicles on the basis of responsibility inherent in the position when the immediate availability of transportation is necessary and approved by HQMC.

b. Submit all requests for class A assignments per this paragraph to the CMC (LFS-2) and include, at a minimum, the following information:

(1) Title or position requiring class A assignment.

(2) Statement of operational conditions that make a class A assignment necessary. In no case will rank or prestige be the sole reason for requesting a class A assignment.

(3) Number and type of vehicles necessary to support the requirement.

c. Authorizations for class A assignments neither provide for nor change vehicle allowance.

d. Authorization for class A assignment does not infer authorization for domicile to place of employment use of the vehicle regardless of residency status (i.e., quarters location in relation to the installation) of the billet incumbent. A class A assignment is neither a prestige assignment nor a waiver of marking and identification requirements. A change in billet incumbents will not require new authorization. Class A authorizations will remain valid until rescinded by HQMC.

3. Class B. This class applies to all GME. Class B assignment authorizes recurring dispatch of the same equipment for activities and functions which by their nature require the use of the same equipment on a daily basis.

a. In all cases, installation commanders will authorize class B assignments in writing and will specify the unit or tenant activity to which assigned.

b. GME fleet managers will initiate an annual review of all class B assignments approved by the installation commander to ensure equipment efficiently supports the official business of the assigned unit or organization.

4. <u>Class C.</u> Fleet managers will pool all GME not assigned under class A or class B authorization for performance of service on an "on-call" basis and to provide equipment for operation of certain scheduled services. On-call dispatches provide services through a single short term dispatch of equipment, usually not longer than a duty day. This includes the dispatch of a pool "taxi vehicle" or providing user operated equipment. This portion of the GME Fleet normally handles the bulk of the installation equipment requirements. This type of service must respond to requirements of an intermittent nature and can consist of ticket or radio dispatch.

2003. <u>OFFICIAL USE OF EQUIPMENT</u>

1. <u>General Information.</u> All GME is for official purposes only. When questions arise concerning the official use of equipment, resolve the issue in favor of strict compliance with the statutory restrictions and the policies of this Manual.

2. <u>Automotive Equipment.</u> The following guidance applies to the official use of automotive equipment.

    a. GME fleet managers may use Marine Corps owned or hired motor vehicles to provide transportation, wholly or in part, for personnel going to or returning from a temporary duty station if official travel orders authorize its use. However, they should make maximum use of public services instead of dispatching vehicles from motor pools. If public or commercial facilities are inadequate or nonexistent, official orders may authorize transportation between lodgings and duty stations for personnel on temporary duty. The temporary duty status of an individual does not necessarily justify the furnishing of transportation by GME. Need, distance involved, and other conditions will determine the use of GME. GME fleet managers will not authorize the use of Government vehicles, hire from General Services Administration (GSA), or commercial rental vehicles in areas serviced by adequate Government bus systems.

    b. Installation commanders may authorize group transportation support for authorized activities such as athletics, welfare, recreation, morale, and chaplains' programs if failure to provide such service would have an adverse effect on the morale of service members, and such transportation is available without detriment to the installation's mission.

    c. GME fleet managers may provide transportation for military and civilian personnel officially participating in public ceremonies; official, social, or civil functions; parades, and military field demonstrations. All non-Government personnel will provide a waiver of liability prior to transport.

    d. Prospective military recruits may receive transportation in connection with interviewing, processing, and orientation.

    e. GME fleet managers will not authorize transportation by Government vehicles for unofficial purposes or cases based solely on reasons of rank, prestige, or personal convenience.

    f. GME fleet managers will not allow the use of motor vehicles, whether authorized on a full-time or trip basis, in support of private business or personal social engagements of the official concerned, family members, or others.

2004. <u>DOMICILE-TO-DUTY</u>. The term "official purpose" will not include transportation, in whole or part, of military personnel or employees between their domiciles and places of employment except in the following cases:

1. <u>The CMC</u>

2. <u>Selected Marine Recruiters</u>. Assignment of an individual to recruiting duty does not, of itself, entitle that individual to receive daily domicile-to-duty transportation. When authorized by the commanding officer, domicile-to-duty transportation may be provided only on days when the individual actually performs field work. Such field work may typically include Marine recruiters who proceed directly from their domicile to conduct official recruiting matters, when it is determined to be infeasible or impractical for the recruiter to first proceed to an office location where the Government motor vehicle is normally garaged.

3. <u>Logs</u>. Marine recruiting stations will maintain local logs or other records for a minimum of 3 years to document the official purpose of all domicile-to-duty transportation.

    a. The logs or records will be easily accessible for audit.

    b. The logs or records will contain the following: name and rank of recruiter using vehicle, name and rank of person authorizing use, passenger carrier identification or registration number, date, location, duration, and circumstances requiring domicile-to-duty transportation.

2005. <u>GROUP TRANSPORTATION SERVICE</u>

1. GME fleet managers will submit requests for authority to establish group transportation services to the CMC (LFS-2). Requests will contain the following information:

a.   Name, mission, and location of the activity.

b.   Current military and civilian strength and authorized changes that will affect transportation requirements.

c.   A description of existing facilities, including the use of privately owned vehicles, car pools, and group riding arrangements.

d.   Points that require service and the distance between the installation and each point.

e.   The number of people requiring recurring transportation between the installation and each point.

f.   A statement describing the efforts made to make existing facilities, public or private, adequate.

g.   The type of service proposed, plus information concerning all necessary arrangements, such as rentals, charters, rates, routes, schedules, type, source, number, seating capacity of the requested equipment, proposed fees, and a map or sketch of the area enclosed. If government-owned vehicles will provide the proposed service, requests must indicate that the local commercial carriers have no desire or capacity to provide the service.

h.   A statement as to the availability of appropriated funds to operate the service.

i.   The desired first date of service.

2.   The following considerations will determine the basis for approval of such services:

a.   Installation so located with respect to the source of manpower that some form of Government assistance is necessary to ensure adequate required transportation for personnel.

b.   In overseas commands where, due to the absence of adequate public or private transportation, local political situations, security, personal safety, or the geographic location of duty station, such transportation is essential to the effective conduct of Government business.

2006.   <u>INSTALLATION OR ACTIVITY BUS SERVICE</u>

1. <u>General Information</u>. The capability to transport groups of individuals on official business between offices or between installations is a recognized requirement and is essential

to mission support. The effective use of buses reduces the requirement for smaller types of passenger carrying equipment at installation motor pools.

2. Scheduled Activity Bus Service

    a. When required to support the defense mission, scheduled bus services may operate within or between installations for the transportation of:

        (1) Enlisted personnel between troop billets and work areas.

        (2) Military personnel and employees between offices and work areas of the installation or activity during normal duty hours.

        (3) Dependents of military personnel on existing scheduled activity routes on a space available basis only, at no cost or inconvenience to the Government. However, GME fleet managers will not establish scheduled activity bus service solely or primarily for dependents to the exclusion of mission requirements, nor may such transportation of dependents generate requirements for additional buses.

    b. Scheduled activity bus service is normally provided with GME. Where local conditions permit and it is more economical to do so, GME fleet managers may request commercial contract service. Installations and activities will use appropriated funds to pay all expenses for the operation of scheduled activity bus services.

    c. Scheduled activity bus service requires careful planning of both routes and schedules. Considerations include the density of population authorized to use such service and activity work schedules. Thorough traffic studies and the working hours of the installation will usually determine the requirement for scheduled activity bus service. Installation commanders will review and approve schedules, at a minimum, on an annual basis.

    d. GME fleet managers will not employ scheduled activity bus service from quarters to work areas for officers residing in assigned quarters or for enlisted personnel residing with their families in family type quarters or other quarters converted for this purpose.

3. Morale, Welfare, and Recreation (MWR) Support Services. GME fleet managers may provide reimbursable bus service in support of authorized MWR programs, Family Service Center Programs, or

private organizations when such mass transportation is available without detriment to the installation's mission. Installations will not use appropriated funds for either the acquisition or lease of group travel vehicles solely or partially to support MWR activities, nor will any reimbursable expenses chargeable for the use of the equipment include any portion of the acquisition cost of the vehicle. Installation commanders may grant approval for this transportation service after considering the potential competition with commercial transportation sources during the decision process. Additionally, it is subject to the following restrictions:

   a. Transportation provided to the following categories on a non-reimbursable basis:

      (1) In support of Chaplain programs.

      (2) MWR functional staffs engaged in routine direct administrative support of category A, B, and C activities. See figure 2-1.

      (3) Teams composed of personnel officially representing the installation in scheduled competitive events.

      (4) DoD personnel or dependent spectators attending local events in which a command or installation-sponsored team is participating.

      (5) Entertainers, guests, supplies, and/or equipment essential to the MWR programs.

      (6) Civilian groups transported to DoD installations in the interest of community relations when invited by the installation commander or other competent authority.

      (7) Category A, B, and C sponsored activities, including recreational tours and trips, when fees are not levied upon the passengers (except fees made to cover the cost of the driver when required) and when approved by the installation commander only after mission requirements have been met.

   b. Special activities such as scouting programs and private organizations may receive transportation on a reimbursable basis covering all operations and maintenance costs of providing the service.

2007. <u>PERMISSIBLE OPERATING DISTANCE (POD)</u>

1. The POD is a guide for determining when it is more economical to use commercial transportation. It is usually more economical

to use the services of commercial carriers for the transportation of personnel and cargo to destinations outside the immediate areas of the installation. Therefore, DoD has established a one-way distance of 100 miles as a guide upon which to base permissible operating distances for motor vehicles. GME fleet managers will make every effort to use commercial transportation outside the POD and GME inside the POD. Use of GME outside the POD requires approval by the owning installation's commander.

2. Each installation will establish a POD and include it in their GME SOP. The POD established for an installation should be sufficient to support normal operations. On the basis of local experience, installations will establish a POD that will adequately support motor vehicle transportation requirements; however, the POD should not normally exceed the distance identified above. Notify the CMC (LFS-2) if the POD exceeds a 100-mile radius.

2008. <u>MINIMUM WALKING DISTANCE</u>

1. A minimum walking distance describes the distance between points of travel beyond which it is reasonable to provide GME for transportation.

2. Each installation's GME SOP will include their minimum walking distance.

2009. <u>TRANSPORTATION OF DEPENDENT SCHOOL CHILDREN</u>

1. <u>Policy</u>. Dependent school children may utilize GME only as specified in this Manual. The preferred equipment will be bus, passenger van, station wagon, or sedan, depending on the number of passengers.

    a. GME fleet managers may provide transportation to dependent school children residing on a Marine Corps installation under any of the three following conditions:

        (1) Local public schools are not accessible.

        (2) Nearby public schools other than the local public schools, when:

            (a) The nearby public school is not accessible.

            (b) Installations may provide transportation to other public schools (to include public schools for the handicapped) within the local educational agency district of residence if determined that local public schools that would normally enroll the children are unable to provide adequately for their education.

(3)   Private schools within a reasonable distance, provided:

(a)   The private school is not accessible and private school transportation, either with or without cost to the child, is not available.

(b)   The parent of the child submits a written request for transportation setting forth the reasons therefore.

(c)   The installation commander concerned determines either that:

1 The local or nearby public schools, if any, are unable to provide adequately for the education of the child concerned.

2 The vehicles authorized for transporting dependent school children to public schools have extra space and can convey those attending private schools without materially deviating from the established route to the public school.

b.   GME fleet managers may provide transportation to dependent school children that do not reside on a Marine Corps installation as follows:

(1)   Dependent school children of military personnel on a space-available basis between schools and military installations only under both of the following criteria:

(a)   The children are participating in a program covered by and implemented in the Uniform Services Health Benefits Program.

(b)   Transportation is already being provided between the military installation and the school concerned.

(c)   The children present themselves at a regular bus stop on the Marine Corps installation or established along the regular route between the military installation and the school.

c.   Children may receive only one trip to and from the school per school day.

d.   When conditions involve more than one Marine Corps installation, GME fleet managers will coordinate transportation arrangements to the maximum extent possible.

e. Pay reimbursable costs to the applicable financial appropriation or fund, or to miscellaneous receipts of the U.S. Treasury, as appropriate. Costs will consist of costs incident to operation, maintenance, and depreciation of equipment, including, but not limited to: fuel, oil, and other consumable supplies used, as well as the compensation of drivers (military or civilian) directly engaged in providing the transportation.

        (1) Compute the compensation rate of civilian drivers on the basis of their gross payroll compensation, plus a factor of 29 percent of gross payroll compensation for fringe benefits.

        (2) Compute the compensation rate of military drivers on the basis of the reimbursement rates for military personnel.

    f. Dependent school children may use available regularly scheduled Marine Corps transportation, within and between installations, when traveling to and from school to make connections with regular means of transportation. Similarly, installation commanders may authorize special transportation within the installation where to do so would serve to make schools accessible by regular means of transportation.

2. Exceptions. The installation commander may, after giving due consideration to the age and maturity of the children involved, grant exceptions when the route to school passes through areas of heavy traffic, blighted urban or residential districts, or potentially dangerous industrial or construction areas.

2010. DETERMINING THE METHOD OF TRANSPORTATION FOR PERSONNEL.
When motor vehicle transportation is essential to the performance of official business and falls outside the minimum walking distance, the following transportation methods apply in the order shown, to the extent that they are available and capable of meeting mission requirements:

1. Marine Corps scheduled bus service.

2. Scheduled public transportation.

3. Marine Corps motor vehicle.

4. Voluntary use of a privately owned motor vehicle on a reimbursable basis.

5. Taxicab, on a reimbursable basis.

2011. <u>UTILIZATION</u>

1. Each installation GME SOP will establish and publish annual utilization goals in terms of a productive index, such as miles driven or passengers or tonnage carried, that will allow effective use of equipment.

2. At least annually, each command will compare actual utilization performance with planned utilization goals for each standard equipment classification and take action to adjust equipment authorizations where utilization performance indicates such action is necessary. GME fleet managers may use any locally devised system that provides this information, however, the following formula is provided as an example:

$$\frac{\text{(actual miles) X (total vehicles)}}{\text{(mileage goal) X (total vehicles)}} = \text{percent utilization}$$

Utilization > 95 percent = Use of equipment is within standards; increase in T/E or assignment is possible.
Utilization > 75 percent = Use of equipment is within standards; increase in T/E or assignment is not possible.
Utilization < 75 percent = Use of equipment is not within standards; decrease in T/E or assignment is possible.

3. Table 2-1 contains the annual utilization goals for each standard equipment classification listed. These goals reflect the anticipated annual mileage for the given GME classification, and validates fleet tables of equipment (T/E) allowances against annual mileage production for each GME fleet.

    a. The usage goals contained in table 2-1 do not apply to class A assignments or special purpose equipment.

    b. GME fleet managers will develop usage goals at the local level for Material Handling Equipment (MHE) and engineer equipment.

2012. <u>LICENSING</u>

1. Each activity will establish a licensing program to meet Federal, State, and local regulations. This program should include a provision requiring out-of-state licensees to read and understand State and local driving regulations including the motor Transport SOP of the dispatching unit.

2. Administrative use commercial automotive equipment (4X2) under 10,000 pounds gross vehicle weight (GVW) requires, as a minimum, a valid State drivers license or Optional Form (OF) 346 (U.S. Government Motor Vehicle Operator's Identification Card). Installation commanders may require other more stringent licensing procedures to meet local rules or requirements.

3. All other GME requires a valid OF 346 containing a rating for the particular equipment. GME fleet managers will issue OF 346's per MCO's 11240.66 and 5110.1, TM 11240-15/3; or, in the case of engineer equipment, TM 11275-15/4.

4. Equipment operators will comply with State and local regulations when operating off installations.

5. GME fleet managers may provide Marine Corps owned motor vehicles to DoD contractors in accordance with contract stipulations. If provided to contractors or subcontractors, contracts will state that such vehicles are for official use only, and will be operated and maintained in accordance with this Manual. DoD contractor personnel do not require the use of OF 346's.

6. Officer Licensing. Officers will not be licensed to drive a government vehicle (commercial or tactical) except for those selected billets which may require an officer to drive. When it is determined that an officer is required to be licensed to operate a government vehicle, the initiation and authorization of licensing action will be given by the installation commander or district director and an entry made in the Officer's Qualification Record. This authorization will be automatically rescinded upon termination of such duty and/or when the officer is transferred. An officer will not routinely drive except in an official duty capacity.

2013. TRAINING

1. Technical training of Marines will be per NAVMC 2779 and MCO 1500.40.

2. GME fleet managers will program and budget for specialized training needed to operate or maintain equipment on hand.

2014. GOVERNMENT TRANSPORTATION IN THE NATIONAL CAPITAL REGION (NCR). DoD and SECNAV policy established specifically for the NCR govern transportation in the NCR.

GARRISON MOBILE EQUIPMENT

Table 2-1.--Annual Utilization Goals.

Equipment	Pounds Gross Vehicle Weight Rating Weight Classification Range	Type	Mileage Standards
Sedan	N/A	All	10,000
Station Wagon	N/A	All	10,000
Bus, Body on Chassis	N/A	All	9,000
Bus, Integral	N/A	All	25,000
Truck, Cargo, Pickup	Under 5,000	4x2	9,000
Truck, Cargo/Multipurpose (including pickups)	Under 10,000	4x4	9,000
		4x2	8,000
Truck, Cargo/Multipurpose	10,000-23,000	4x2	8,000
		4x4	7,000
		6x4	6,000
Truck, Cargo/Multipurpose	Over 23,000	All	7,000
Truck, Carryall	N/A	All	9,000
Truck, Tractor	Under 25,000	All	7,000
Truck, Tractor	25,000-46,000	4x2	7,000
		4x4	6,000
		6x6	5,000
Truck, Tractor	Over 46,000	6x4	6,000
		6x6	5,000
Motorcycle	N/A	All	3,000
Scooter, 3 or 4 Wheeled	N/A	Gasoline	2,000

NOTE: There are no suggested standards for material handling equipment (MHE) and engineer equipment. GME fleet managers will establish local utilization standards for all GME MHE and engineer equipment.

Category A - Mission Sustaining Activities

Armed Forces Professional Entertainment Program Overseas
Common Support Services
Gymnasium/Physical Fitness/Aquatic Training
Libraries
Parks and Picnic Areas
Recreation Centers/Rooms
Shipboard/Isolated/Deployed/Free Admission Motion Pictures
Sports/Athletics (Self-Directed, Unit Level, Intramural)
Unit Level Programs and Activities
Temporary Lodging Facility (In support of official travel)

Category B - Community Support Activities

Arts and Crafts Skill Development
Automotive Crafts Skill Development
Child Development Centers
Entertainment (Music and Theater)
Outdoor Recreation
Recreational Swimming Pools
Sports Programs (Above the intramural level)
Youth Activities
Stars and Stripes
Bowling Centers (12 lanes or less)
Joint Service Facility
Marinas without Resale or Private Boat Berthing
Recreation Equipment Checkout
Recreational Information, Tickets, and Tour Services

Category C - Business Activities

Aero Clubs
Amusement Machine Locations and Centers
Animal Care Funds
Armed Services Exchange and Related Activities
Armed Forces Recreation Centers (Accommodation/dining and resale
facilities)
Audio/Photo and Other Resale Activities
Bingo
Bowling Centers (over 12 lanes)
Cabins/Cottages/Cabanas/Recreational Guest Houses
Catering
Civilian Dining, Vending, and Other Resale Activities and Services

Figure 2-1.--Categories of MWR Activities.

2-17

Golf Courses
Marinas and Boating Activities with Resale or Private Boat
Berthing
Military Open Messes/Clubs
Motion Pictures (Paid admission function)
Motorcycle Clubs
Package Stores
Parachute/Sky Diving Clubs
Rod and Gun Clubs
Skating Rinks
Skeet/Trap Ranges
Snack Bars/Soda Fountain
Stables
Supplemental Mission Funds (In-flight services/military museums,
etc.)
Temporary Lodging Facility
Unofficial Commercial Travel Services

Figure 2-1.--Categories of MWR Activities--Continued.

GARRISON MOBILE EQUIPMENT

CHAPTER 3

PROCUREMENT

FIGURE

CHAPTER 3

PROCUREMENT

3000. <u>GENERAL INFORMATION</u>. A major objective of the GME program
is to achieve the optimum relationship between equipment
investment costs and the productive use of essential task suited
equipment. Allowances represent not only authorizations to hold
equipment but also serve as a procurement goal. The total number
of GME items in use at any command, including government-owned or
long-term leased, may not exceed allowances established by HQMC.

3001. <u>BUDGETING</u>. The CMC (LFS-2) budgets Procurement, Marine
Corps (PMC) funds for procurement of all centrally managed
appropriated funded GME. Three factors determine budgeting:

1. Allowances.

2. On hand inventory.

3. Projected retirement year.

3002. <u>PROCUREMENT CYCLE</u>

1. The annual procurement cycle is as follows:

Fiscal Year Begins.

Oct   The CMC (LFS-2) sends Annual GME Inventory Audit Report
         and listing of procurements scheduled for new fiscal
         year to GME fleet managers.

Nov   GME fleet managers return GME Inventory Audit Reports to
         the CMC (LFS-2) along with past fiscal year utilization
         data.

Dec-Mar The CMC (LFS-2) projects procurements for next fiscal
         year.

Jun   Projected procurements for next fiscal year sent to GME
         fleet managers.

Jun   GME fleet managers submit their Local Procurement Status
         Report (as applicable) to the CMC (LFS-2).

Jul   GME fleet managers submit priorities and acquisition data
         for next fiscal year procurements to the CMC (LFS-2).

Jul-Oct The CMC (LFS-2) prepares Funding Action Requests (FAR),
         Military Interdepartmental Purchase Requests (MIPR's),
         and allotments prepared for next fiscal year procurement.

Cycle begins again.

2.   The Annual GME Inventory Audit reflects current and projected
serialized allowances and validates each GME fleet.

3.   The Projected Procurement Letter, sent to GME fleet managers
in March, identifies all equipment tentatively scheduled for
replacement during the upcoming fiscal year. GME fleet managers
will review and return this letter, including any proposed
substitutions or additions to the projected procurement, and a
priority designator for each item listed. Additionally, they
will submit GME Ordering Data Sheets to inform the CMC (LFS-2) of
any nonstandard specifications required to meet their operational
needs. Figure 3-1 contains an example.

4.   GME fleet managers will note any requirement for a service
representative for training purposes on any procurement
specification, whether local or centrally managed.

3003.   PROCUREMENT METHODS

1.   Centralized Procurement. Centralized procurement is the
primary method in which HQMC achieves significant cost savings by
consolidating Marine Corps GME acquisition requirements with
other Department of Defense (DoD) components.

2.   Local Procurement. Local procurement is appropriate when
circumstances are such that centralized procurement will provide
no fiscal advantage or when the urgency of the situation so
dictates. When authorized, the CMC (LFS-2) will allot PMC funds
to GME fleet managers for local procurement of assets. When
using local procurement, it is imperative that GME fleet managers
make every effort to obtain a contract as expeditiously as
possible consistent with good contracting practice. GME fleet
managers will inform the CMC (LFS-2) of the status of any fiscal
year local GME procurement allotments in letter format by 30 June
each year. This letter will include all authorized local GME
procurements involving PMC funds, and the status of those funds.
Figure 3-2 provides an example Local Procurement Status Report
letter (this report is exempt from reports control).

3004. <u>ALLOWANCES</u>

1. Published Table of Equipment allowances maintain the minimum GME assets required at each Marine Corps activity or command to provide essential services under normal conditions. GME fleet managers may, as necessary, borrow assets from other Marine Corps activities, other DoD activities, other governmental agencies, or lease from GSA or commercial sources to meet peak loads and other unusual requirements for GME. The total number of GME items in use at any command, including government-owned or long-term leased, may not exceed allowances established by HQMC. GME fleet managers may exceed their T/E allowance only through short-term leases or by temporarily loaning selected equipment from other GME accounts.

2. GME fleet managers will request allowance modifications from the CMC (LFS-2). The request will include the following:

    a. T/E number.

    b. Equipment code requiring modification.

    c. Current allowances.

    d. Requested allowance.

    e. Detailed justification addressing the entire allowance and usage data for that equipment code, including why the current allowance is inadequate to meet new needs.

    f. Any other equipment allowances affected.

3005. <u>SEDAN AUTHORIZATIONS</u>

1. The DoD requires all commercial type motor vehicles acquired within the DoD to be the minimum body size, maximum fuel efficiency, and minimum ancillary equipment necessary to fulfill the operational mission for which obtained. Additionally, the Marine Corps will acquisition, whether by purchase or by lease, only class II (compact) sedans except when the CMC approves class III (mid-size) sedans as mission essential. Accordingly, GME fleet managers will satisfy requirement using class II (compact) sedans, except for the following:

    a. The CMC.

    b. The CMC may authorize the lease of class III (mid-size) sedans for use by commanding generals and their deputies of installations or major commands when the officer holding that billet is a general officer. Commanding officers of major installations may request authorization for class III (mid-size) sedans only when they are responsible for the overall protocol functions of that installation.

2. Commands will request letters of authorization for leasing class III (mid-size) sedans from the CMC (LFS-2) and must possess authorization prior to making any lease arrangements.

3. Funding for the lease of CMC authorized class III vehicles is the responsibility of the command concerned using local O&M,MC funds. Under no circumstances will the Marine Corps procure class III mid-size sedans.

4. Upon issue of a letter of authorization for a class III (mid-size) sedan, the CMC (LFS-2) will replace GME fleet T/E allowances for class II (compact) sedans with an allowance for leased class III (mid-size) sedan of the same quantity.

5. Law Enforcement Sedans. This Headquarters will lease only class III (mid-size) law enforcement sedans or suitable replacements to satisfy requirements for law enforcement sedans. GME fleet managers may modify the vehicle at their expense for particular law enforcement requirements above the basic package as required.

3006. USED EQUIPMENT

1. The procurement of used serviceable equipment is an economical alternate method of filling GME requirements but does not constitute a primary source of equipment.

2. When a GME fleet manager becomes aware of a serviceable used item that will fill a particular requirement, the manager should notify the CMC (LFS-2) in writing and include a full description of the equipment, approximate cost, and information regarding equipment it replaces and allowances affected.

3. If approved, the CMC (LFS-2) will obtain appropriate waivers from single item managers and forward local purchase authority and funding to the requesting GME fleet manager.

GARRISON MOBILE EQUIPMENT

```
Equip Code _____      Description _____
FY Qty Desired _____      Activity _____   T/E No. _____
                           Automotive
Markings:

Cooling System:

Towing Devices:

Exhaust:

Tailgate:

Drive Wheels:

Engine:

Auxiliary Engine:

Heater/Air-Conditioner:

Fuel Tank:

Transmission:

Differential:

Power Takeoff:

Tires:

Brakes:

Accessories:

Bed:

Boom/Hoist/Winch:

Racks/Cabinets:

Payload:

Delivery Instructions:

Other Requirements:
```

Figure 3-1.--GME Ordering Data Sheet.

GARRISON MOBILE EQUIPMENT

```
 _____
| Equip Code _____    Description _____ |
| FY Qty Desired _____    Activity _____  T/E No. _____ |
|             Material Handling Equipment                  |
| Engine/Power Source:                                     |
| Safety Cutout:                                           |
| Width/Height:                                            |
| Mast:                                                    |
| Load Backrest:                                           |
| Tires:                                                   |
| Brakes:                                                  |
| Towing Device:                                           |
| Sling/Tie-down:                                          |
| Controls and Instrumentation:                            |
| Markings:                                                |
| Transmission:                                            |
| Hydraulics:                                              |
| Forks:                                                   |
| Battery Charger:                                         |
| Draw-bar Pull:                                           |
| Turning Radius/Steering:                                 |
| Winch/Boom:                                              |
| Accessories:                                             |
| Delivery Instructions:                                   |
| Other Requirements:                                      |
|_____|
```

Figure 3-1.--GME Ordering Data Sheet--Continued.

```
┌─────────────────────────────────────────────────────────────────┐
│ Equip Code _____      Description _____   │
│ FY Qty Desired _____      Activity _____  T/E No. _____   │
│                    Engineer Equipment                             │
│                                                                   │
│ Engine/Power Source:                                              │
│                                                                   │
│ Cooling System:                                                   │
│                                                                   │
│ Fuel Tank:                                                        │
│                                                                   │
│ Transmission:                                                     │
│                                                                   │
│ Steering:                                                         │
│                                                                   │
│ Tracks/Wheels/Tires:                                             │
│                                                                   │
│ Electrical System/Battery:                                       │
│                                                                   │
│ Accessories:                                                      │
│                                                                   │
│ Towing Devices/Draw-bar Pull:                                    │
│                                                                   │
│ Air-Conditioner/Heater:                                          │
│                                                                   │
│ Hydraulics:                                                       │
│                                                                   │
│ Instruments/Controls:                                            │
│                                                                   │
│ Winch/Hoist/Power Takeoff:                                       │
│                                                                   │
│ Blade/Ripper/Backhoe:                                            │
│                                                                   │
│ Color/Markings:                                                  │
│                                                                   │
│ Pumps:                                                            │
│                                                                   │
│ Sling/Tie-down:                                                  │
│                                                                   │
│ Brakes:                                                           │
│                                                                   │
│ Operating Weight/Capacity:                                       │
│                                                                   │
│ Delivery Instructions:                                           │
│                                                                   │
│ Other Requirements:                                              │
└─────────────────────────────────────────────────────────────────┘
```

Figure 3-1.--GME Ordering Data Sheet--Continued.

From:
To: Commandant of the Marine Corps (LFS), Headquarters,
        U.S. Marine Corps, 2 Navy Annex, Washington,
        DC 20380-1775

Subj: STATUS OF FY__ LOCAL PROCUREMENT

Ref: (a) MCO P11240.106B

1. As required by the reference, the following information is
provided:

    a. Total Funds Authorized: $_____

    b. Procured Items

    Item   Funds   Actual
Authorized   Authorized   Procurement Cost

1.
2.
3.
                     _____   _____
Total Procurement Requirement $ (Excess or Deficiency)

    c. Pending Procurements

    Item   Funds   Actual
Authorized   Authorized   Procurement Cost

1.
2.
3.

    d. Items Authorized and Not Procured
                                              Remarks
    Item   Funds   (Justification for
Description   Authorized   Not Procuring)

1.
2.
3.

Total unobligated $_____
(Total Excess or Total Deficient)

Figure 3-2.-- Example Local Procurement Status Report.

GARRISON MOBILE EQUIPMENT

CHAPTER 4

LEASING

CHAPTER 4

LEASING

4000. __GENERAL INFORMATION__. The three methods of leasing available to GME fleet managers are short-term, long-term, and Vehicle Lease Program (VLP).

1. __Short-Term__. Local commanders may approve short-term leases of any item of GME for periods less than 60 days. Funding short-term leases remains the responsibility of the installation. Short-term leases are not renewable. GME fleet managers should consider short-term leases to satisfy unscheduled or nonrecurring requirements where Marine Corps-owned equipment is not available for use or cannot economically meet operational demands. Short-term leases may temporarily increase the on-hand vehicle quantities beyond the approved T/E.

2. __Long-Term.__ A long-term lease is of 60 days duration or longer. The installation must have either a T/E deficiency in Marine Corps-owned equipment or an expected need for a specific duration. Funding long-term leases remains the responsibility of the installation. GME fleet managers should consider long-term lease allowances when assets on hand have consistently accumulated high usage data and a comparison of costs indicates a replacement by leased equipment would provide a cost advantage over continued use of a Marine Corps-owned equipment.

    a. GME fleet managers will request long-term leases per paragraph 4001, below, and report long-term automotive leases to the CMC per paragraph 4005, below.

    b. Long-term leasing of GME assets requires approval from the CMC. Status of scheduled procurements, and the availability of GSA-leased equipment, are primary considerations for approving long-term lease.

3. __VLP__. Recent changes to Public Law mandated a study by DoD into methods by which it could improve its commercial vehicle fleet and reduce its operational costs. This study resulted in the VLP. The VLP consists of long-term leases of automotive GME assets by HQMC using Operation and Maintenance Marine Corps (OMMC) funds rather than procurements with Procurement Marine Corps (PMC) funds. This provides GME fleet managers with a substantially newer GME vehicle fleet operating at reduced maintenance costs, and permits the Marine Corps to take full advantage of emerging automotive technologies.

4001. <u>LONG-TERM LEASE REQUEST PROCEDURES</u>. GME fleet managers will submit requests for long-term leases to the CMC (LFS-2). Requests must include the following:

1. Number of items of equipment required by type.

2. Specific and detailed justification of need for lease.

3. Estimated individual cost per month per item, and total monthly cost for all items.

4. Anticipated period of lease.

5. Justification for maintenance by Marine Corps maintenance facilities instead of contractor-provided maintenance.

4002. <u>ADMINISTRATION OF LEASED EQUIPMENT</u>

1. <u>Contracts</u>. Leasing GME with appropriated funds must follow the policies set forth in the Federal Acquisition Regulation, the Federal Property Management Regulation, and other current directives.

2. GME fleet managers will operate all leased equipment, including short-term, long-term, and VLP vehicles, in the same manner as prescribed for Marine Corps-owned equipment unless otherwise specified in the contract.

3. <u>Responsibility and Liability.</u> Using units are responsible and liable for damage and injuries incurred during the operation of leased vehicles and equipment in the same manner as Marine Corps-owned equipment and vehicles.

4. GME fleet managers will not purchase vehicle insurance for leased vehicles as the Government is self-insured.

5. The contractor will perform all maintenance on leased equipment when practical, unless the GME fleet manager makes a prior determination that it will be more economical for the Marine Corps to perform such maintenance in whole or in part.

6. Local commanders will budget O&M,MC funds for short- and long-term leases of commercial equipment per MCO P7100.8. The CMC (LFS-2) will budget for VLP vehicles.

7. Status of scheduled procurements, and the availability of GSA-leased equipment, are primary considerations for approving long-term leases. Marine Corps Air Station (MCAS) Iwakuni, and

Marine Corps Base (MCB) Camp Butler locally procure GME. Since GSA-leased equipment is not available in Western Pacific (WestPac), the commanders of these installations have authority to approve long-term leases of GME. GME fleet managers of these installations will report long-term leases per paragraph 4005, below.

8. Sedan size limitations of Marine Corps-owned vehicles apply to all leased equipment, including short-term, long-term, and VLP vehicles.

4003. <u>MARKING LEASED EQUIPMENT</u>. With the following exceptions, chapter 6 of this Manual contains the policy for marking all leased equipment and VLP vehicles.

1. GME fleet managers will not mark short-term lease equipment.

2. GME fleet managers will not affix USMC registration numbers to either long-term leased vehicles or VLP vehicles.

3. Long-term leasing of equipment specifically exempted by HQMC from displaying identification markings will not have markings installed.

4. The application of markings on equipment and removal of such markings is, like other factors of the contract, subject to the agreement between the furnishing agency and the activity making the leasing arrangements. GME fleet managers will consider using magnetic or other temporary methods for applying required markings to preclude added costs of removal.

4004. <u>T/E ALLOWANCES FOR LEASED EQUIPMENT.</u> Either the GME fleet manager or HQMC may determine that long-term recurring leasing rather than procurement may be more economical for certain equipment. When this is the case, the CMC (LFS-2) will authorize a T/E allowance specifically for leased equipment thereby eliminating the need to renew leasing authority.

4005. <u>LONG-TERM LEASE</u> REPORT (REPORT CONTROL SYMBOL DN-11240-01). Fleet managers will submit an annual report in letter format by 31 October to the CMC containing all long-term leases of equipment during the previous fiscal year. Figure 4-1 contains a sample format.

```
From:
To:     Commandant of the Marine Corps (LFS), Headquarters, U.S.
        Marine Corps, 2 Navy Annex, Washington, DC  20380-1775

Subj:   LONG-TERM LEASE REPORT

Ref:    (a) MCO P11240.106

1.  In accordance with the reference, the following provides
information pertaining to this installation's long-term leases:

T/E:_____


                                    Lease     Lease     Total
Equipment                           Start     End       No.
Nomenclature        TAMCN           Date      Date      Days


_____         _____       _____     _____     _____


Total           Total
Lease             No.
Cost          Miles/Hrs

_____         _____
```

Figure 4-1.--Long-Term Lease Report.

4-6

GARRISON MOBILE EQUIPMENT

CHAPTER 5

SAFETY, ACCIDENT PREVENTION, AND REPORTING

GARRISON MOBILE EQUIPMENT

CHAPTER 5

SAFETY, ACCIDENT PREVENTION, AND REPORTING

5000. GENERAL INFORMATION

1. Accidents involving Marine Corps equipment impose an alarming drain on Marine Corps resources. To avoid these losses, all GME fleet managers will conduct an aggressive and continuing safety program.

2. The Marine Corps emphasizes accident prevention programs so as to stimulate safety consciousness. GME fleet managers will develop accident prevention programs at all levels to ensure operators of vehicles and equipment are knowledgeable of recognized safety and accident prevention practices. These programs will, at a minimum, include the following:

    a. Specific written guidelines for the safe operation of motor vehicles, equipment, and all ancillary attachments.

    b. Equipment safety education, orientation, and observance of recognized safety practices.

    c. Periodic equipment safety inspections.

    d. Reporting, investigation, and analysis of equipment accidents.

    e. Appropriate action against safety violators.

3. The GME fleet managers will maintain necessary liaison with civil authorities within their area of operation and ensure that operators are familiar with civil laws, rules, and regulations on motor vehicle operations.

5001. ACCIDENTS

1. Prior to operation of a Marine Corps-owned or -leased vehicle, operators will ensure that SF 91 (Operators' Report of Motor Vehicle Accident) is available and carried in the vehicle.

2. Operators involved in accidents will:

    a. Stop immediately.

    b. Render any possible assistance to the injured. Avoid moving any seriously injured persons unless essential for their protection.

    c. Warn other motorists of any existing highway hazard. During hours of darkness or poor visibility, use flares or reflectors.

    d. Notify civil and military police authorities after taking above action.

    e. Complete SF 91. If the driver is unable to complete the SF 91 due to injury or death, the next senior person directly responsible for equipment operations will complete the report.

    f. Comply with State and local laws governing the reporting of equipment accidents.

    g. Not leave accident scene until advised to do so by proper authority.

    h. Not express opinions (orally or in writing) to claimants or their agents as to liability, investigation findings, or the possibility of a claim approval.

    i. Obtain clearance from the claims officer prior to delivery of an accident report to a third party. This includes State or local officials. Drivers will not make official accident investigation reports available to a claimant, or to any individual or representative of any non-Marine Corps organization.

    j. Complete DD Form 518 (Accident-Identification Card) at the scene of the accident or as promptly as possible thereafter and provide copies to persons directly concerned with the accident. DD Form 518 provides any person involved in an accident with all of the information they require of the equipment operator.

    k. As soon as possible thereafter, deliver the completed SF 91 to the GME fleet manager.

3. GME fleet managers will take appropriate action against operators if they fail to report any accidents.

5002. <u>INVESTIGATION AND REPORTING OF ACCIDENTS</u>

1. GME fleet managers will initiate an investigation for each accident involving Marine Corps owned or leased equipment and make a determination concerning the cause(s) and surrounding circumstances, including how to prevent a reoccurrence.

2. GME fleet managers will ensure mishap and hazard reports are completed per MCO P5102.1.

5003. <u>EQUIPMENT OPERATOR'S MANUAL.</u> The equipment operator's manual contains information pertaining to the safe operation of equipment. GME fleet managers will conduct sufficient operator training to ensure operators are familiar with and adhere to this information.

5004. <u>SAFETY INSPECTIONS</u>. Equipment supervisors will conduct annual safety inspections for all items of GME per the procedures outlined in paragraph 7002.2 of this Manual. Induct equipment that is unsafe for operation into the supporting maintenance facility.

5005. <u>SEATBELTS</u>. Vehicle operators and passengers will properly use and wear seatbelts when operating or riding in any GME so equipped. Three point belts (cross-chest shoulder strap) will be worn with the cross-chest strap properly positioned across the wearer's chest. To the extent possible, personnel shall be transported in vehicles such as sedans, station wagons, vans, or buses. Occupants shall be seated when the vehicle is in motion. Personnel may be transported without fixed seats for short distances on the installation if each passenger remains seated wholly in the body of the vehicle.

5006. <u>SMOKING</u>. There will be no smoking of any tobacco products in any GME.

5007. <u>RATED CAPACITY.</u> GME fleet managers will take steps to ensure that GME does not operate above or beyond its rated capacity.

5008. <u>CELL PHONES</u>. Operators of GME will not use cellular phones while the equipment is in motion.

GARRISON MOBILE EQUIPMENT

CHAPTER 6

REGISTRATION, IDENTIFICATION, AND MARKING

6-1

GARRISON MOBILE EQUIPMENT

CHAPTER 6

REGISTRATION, IDENTIFICATION, AND MARKING

6000. <u>REGISTRATION NUMBER ASSIGNMENT</u>

1. Each centrally managed GME item has a Marine Corps registration number assigned by HQMC for the purpose of establishing permanent and positive identification. Paragraph 6001, below, describes non-appropriated fund vehicle registration. Once assigned, the registration number remains the same for the life of the equipment or until permanent transfer from Marine Corps custody. In no case will GME fleet managers either change or reassign registration numbers with another vehicle.

2. Low-cost or short life-expectancy equipment funded for by the CMC (LFS-2), but is not centrally managed, will not receive registration numbers.

3. There are two types of GME registration numbers: the first type applies to all GME held against a T/E allowance regardless of the source of the equipment. The second type of registration number (with an "X" in the middle) applies to all equipment held by non-T/E accounts (Commissaries, MWR, Forestry) which do not have a T/E allowance regardless of the source or type of funds used to procure the equipment. Paragraph 6001, below, describes non-appropriated fund (NAF) vehicle registration.

4. When equipment bearing tactical registration numbers is redesignated as GME to fill temporary T/E deficiencies, GME fleet managers will report the equipment using the tactical registration number.

6001. <u>NONAPPROPRIATED FUND VEHICLE REGISTRATION</u>. GME fleet managers will register all transportation equipment for NAF activities, whether received from excess GME, Defense Reutilization and Marketing Office (DRMO), or by procurement, with "X" type series registration numbers. The legend "for official use only" will not appear. However, the identification will include the name of the using activity (e.g., Marine Corps Community Services, etc.) on the vehicle. To obtain USMC NAF registration numbers for MWR vehicles, GME fleet managers may submit requests to: Personal and Family Readiness Division, Headquarters U.S. Marine Corps (MRB-1), 3044 Catlin Avenue, Quantico, VA 22134.

6002. PAINTING AND DECALS

1. Marine Corps-owned Vehicles and Equipment. GME fleet
managers will repaint Marine Corps-owned GME only to restore
adequate protection against rust or corrosion. They will not
repaint equipment merely to improve appearance, or to change the
color or gloss characteristics if the finish is serviceable. The
preferred standard paint scheme for GME vehicles is standard
commercial vehicle manufacturing industry white paint; however,
GME fleet managers may use suitable substitute colors to achieve
economy. Paint MHE and engineer equipment per Federal Standard
895, yellow number 13538.

2. Leased Vehicles and Equipment. GME fleet managers will not
paint leased vehicles or equipment, including short-term, long-
term, or VLP vehicles, to conform to the standard white GME paint
scheme. The only identification markings that any leased vehicle
will display is State license plates and any such window decals
required by State or local authority.

3. Decals. GME fleet managers will affix only such additional
decals or placards to GME assets as required to ensure the safe
operation of the equipment.

    a. All Leased Vehicles and Equipment. GME fleet managers
will not affix decals, magnetic signs, etc., to any portion of
the painted surface or the chromium-plated trim of short-term
leased vehicles or equipment. Placement and removal of decals on
long-term leased vehicles and equipment, and VLP vehicles, will
be subject to the agreement between the leasor and the agency
furnishing the vehicles.

    b. Recruiters. Recruiters may place appropriate advertising
slogans on the side windows of vehicles as long as such decals do
not interfere with the driver's vision or the safe operation of
the vehicle.

6003. IDENTIFICATION MARKINGS FOR MOTOR VEHICLES

1. General. This section contains policies and procedures for
the marking of GME motor vehicles. GME fleet managers will not
change the existing identification and markings presently affixed
to vehicles to coincide with this policy. Upon permanent
disposal of a vehicle, they will remove or obliterate all vehicle
identification.

2. Prescribed Identification. Short-term lease vehicles
require only a standard State license plate for the location of
the lease. All long-term leased vehicles will display either a

GSA, State, or U. S. government license plate mounted on the front and rear of the vehicle. All VLP vehicles will display a GSA license plate mounted on the front and rear of the vehicle. Two wheeled vehicles will display a license plate on the rear of the vehicle only. State and GSA license plates are standard as issued. The U.S. government license plates will contain the following:

    a. License plates will consist of dark blue figures on a white background.

    b. The top line will consist of "U.S. GOVERNMENT" printed with 1/2 inch capital gothic letters placed centered 1/2 inch from the top of the license plate.

    c. The center line will consist of "M" centered over "C" in 1-inch capital gothic letters. Immediately to the right will be the six-digit USMC registration number of the vehicle. Format the center line such that the top edge of the "M" is level with the top edge of the USMC registration number, while the lower edge of the "C" is level with the lower edge of the USMC registration number. The entire center line will appear centered on the license plate 1/2 inch below the top line.

    d. The bottom line will consist of "OFFICIAL USE ONLY" printed in 1/2 inch capital gothic letters placed centered 1/2 inch from the bottom of the license plate.

6004. <u>IDENTIFICATION MARKINGS FOR MATERIAL HANDLING EQUIPMENT</u>

1. Affix identification markings on each side and rear, using 1-1/2-inch lettering and numerals. Locate markings where space will permit and in such a manner as to present a neat and balanced appearance. The location of markings will be consistent on equipment of the same type, size, and design.

2. Identification markings will include the letters "USMC" followed by the registration number on the same line (e.g., USMC 000000).

3. Apply identification markings with black paint (No. 17038) when using paint and stencils. GME fleet managers should make maximum use of pressure sensitive marking materials conforming to the current issue of military specification MIL-M-43719. Ensure any attachments do not wholly or partially obscure markings.

6005. <u>IDENTIFICATION MARKINGS FOR ENGINEER EQUIPMENT</u>. GME fleet managers will not mark short-term leased engineer equipment.

Mark Marine Corps-owned and long-term leased equipment as follows:

1. Side Markings

    a. Centered on each front door, or in a comparable position in relation to the driver's seat on equipment without doors.

    b. Trailers and Semitrailers: Centered on each side of the front quarter of the vehicle.

    c. Scooters/Generators/Other Equipment: Located on appropriate surface.

2. Rear Markings. Display only "UNITED STATES MARINE CORPS" and registration number.

3. Size, Space, and Style of Markings. Use 3-inch gothic style letters and numerals except for "Official Use Only" which uses 3/4-inch gothic style letters. Line spacing will be 1-1/2 inches.

4. Use of Pressure Sensitive Marking Materials. GME fleet managers will make maximum use of pressure sensitive type markers for all identification markings prescribed by this chapter.

6006. EXEMPTIONS FROM IDENTIFICATION AND MARKING

1. The following categories of vehicles are exempt from identification and markings:

    a. Motor vehicles used by the CMC. Vehicles will display official U.S. Government license plates or State of Virginia license plates.

    b. Motor vehicles used for investigative or security purposes, or those required to be unidentified under the conditions of a Status of Forces Agreement.

2. The exemption applies only to exterior markings and identification of Marine Corps vehicles. Fleet managers will mark exempt vehicles by painting the USMC registration number on both the underside of the trunk lid and on the inner side of the glove compartment lid. In lieu of painting, Fleet managers may affix either a plastic or corrosion resistant metal plate stamped with the registration number in either of these two prescribed locations.

3. Fleet managers will submit requests for identification and marking exemptions to the CMC (LFS-2).

4. Exempt vehicles utilizing State license plates will adhere to all State and local regulations and procedures for obtaining State license plates. GME fleet managers will fund for obtaining and maintenance of State license plates.

GARRISON MOBILE EQUIPMENT

CHAPTER 7

MAINTENANCE MANAGEMENT

GARRISON MOBILE EQUIPMENT

CHAPTER 7

MAINTENANCE MANAGEMENT

7000. <u>GENERAL INFORMATION</u>

1. GME fleet managers will establish an efficient, well planned, and economical program for the inspection, service, adjustment, and lubrication of all GME assigned to their installation. This program will provide optimum maintenance at the greatest cost effectiveness. The objective of the maintenance program is to perform only that essential maintenance during the normal life expectancy as is required to retain equipment in a safe and serviceable condition, and in an acceptable appearance. In establishing, operating, or managing any maintenance program, GME fleet managers will ensure that their efforts produce an efficient and economically sound operation.

2. Fleet Managers will use the following general guidance in establishing a maintenance program:

    a. The operator's skill, care, attitude, and pride are of primary importance in prolonging the life of equipment. It is the operator's responsibility to ascertain that the equipment is in a safe and serviceable operating condition. Simple operational services and checks with prompt reporting of deficiencies to appropriate supervisory personnel will best maintain equipment in a safe, ready-to-use condition.

    b. Establish scheduled maintenance services on the basis of mileage or hours, manufacturers' standard recommendations, and experience. Other considerations include the age of equipment, local operating requirements, conditions, terrain, and climate.

    c. GME fleet managers will determine the most suitable system (automated or manual) for control of their equipment maintenance, and collection of pertinent data. Systems will be compatible with Headquarters Marine Corps reporting requirements. When using DD, NAVMC, or SF forms, prepare them per TM 4700-15/1. Local commanders may authorize their GME fleet managers to use locally devised forms that provide the same level of control, management capability, and utility.

7001. <u>MAINTENANCE CATEGORIES</u>

1. <u>Operator Inspection and Service</u>. Operator inspection and service will consist of inspection and detection of such

malfunctions of the equipment that could render the unit unsafe or unserviceable. In addition, operator service may include minor or simple parts replacement and servicing (i.e., water, fuel, air, tires, and battery) as required. In cases where other designated personnel service the equipment, the operator will retain responsibility for verifying the completion of services and that the equipment is in a safe and serviceable condition. The operator inspection and service will include, but not be restricted to, the sample checklist in figure 7-1.

2. Safety Inspection. All Marine Corps-owned automotive equipment will receive an annual safety inspection. Where required, GME fleet managers may shorten the safety inspection interval to meet State or local regulations. At a minimum, the annual safety inspection will include the manufacturer's recommended safety inspection. Maintenance facilities will correct noted deficiencies and annotate any maintenance performed on a Shop Repair Order (SRO), or comparable form, before returning the equipment to use. GSA and other leased vehicles will receive a safety inspection as directed by the leasor.

3. Corrective Maintenance (CM). The CM is the total of the maintenance actions performed, as a result of a failure, to restore an item of equipment to a serviceable condition. The CM process commences when any individual reports an item of equipment as requiring CM. It terminates when maintenance actions restore the item to a serviceable condition or determine repairs are not economically feasible.

4. Scheduled Maintenance (SM)

    a. The SM is the sum of the actions taken to maintain equipment in a serviceable condition. This includes providing systematic inspections, to detect potential failures before they occur, or to correct failures before they develop into major defects. A systematic SM program of inspecting, cleaning, servicing, lubricating, and adjusting is the key to equipment readiness in a unit. SM is normally conducted by using unit operators and owning unit mechanics. A good SM program will help prevent early breakdown or failure of equipment, thus assisting in preventing costly, complex, and time-consuming repairs. A sound SM program also optimizes maintenance resources. The SM services are cyclic in nature based on usage or time intervals. SM is often referred to as preventive maintenance (PM).

    b. Service Managers will inspect and service equipment per time or usage intervals prescribed by the manufacturer to maintain the validity of the warranty. They will continue to use the recommended intervals after the warranty expires. Service checks will include all checks indicated by the manufacturer. If there are no intervals prescribed to maintain the warranty, perform scheduled services every 12 months or 5,000 miles for light automotive equipment, 12,000 for medium and heavy automotive equipment, and 12 months or 250 hours for MHE and engineer equipment. GME fleet managers may shorten the interval at their discretion.

7002. CONTROL

1. The economy and soundness of managing equipment maintenance are contingent upon proper and adequate controls instituted at all levels of command. To meet the primary objectives of the maintenance program, it is essential that commanders ensure that the activity maintenance programs take cognizance of maintenance requirements of GME.

2. Controls established by GME fleet managers will provide for:

   a. Minimum equipment downtime to allow maximum equipment availability.

   b. Balanced and meaningful workload scheduling.

   c. Meaningful quality control.

   d. Current equipment technical library.

   e. Appropriate recordkeeping that avoids duplicate efforts.

3. To ensure effective control over shop productivity, the application of flat rate time standards is necessary. Commercial flat rate manuals contain this information.

7003. MAINTENANCE PROCEDURES

1. GME fleet managers may use the following alternative methods or combination of methods to accomplish maintenance actions:

   a. Organic facilities (to include in-house contract maintenance).

   b. Other Government facilities.

   c. Commercial facilities.

2. Regardless of the method selected for maintenance, qualified inspector personnel assigned to the installation or activity will perform a quality insurance inspection prior to returning the vehicle to service. In cases of host-tenant occupancy of an

activity, the host service will perform the maintenance support consistent with practices established for maintenance of its own vehicles unless otherwise specified in support agreements.

3.   The GME fleet managers will establish and use performance standards to evaluate maintenance facilities. These may be any or all of the following, depending on the commander's needs:

    a.   Comparison of vehicle out of service time (downtime) to an established standard.

    b.   Comparison of cost per mile, hour, or unit to the established standard for the installation.

    c.   Comparison of actual man-hours per 1,000 miles (operating hour or unit) to an established standard for a group of like equipment.

    d.   Comparison of shop performance productivity using actual productive hours compared to available hours for a given time period.

    e.   Comparison of direct labor hours to indirect labor hours.

    f.   Comparison of individual performance against a flat rate or other established time standard.

4.   GME fleet managers will set forth instructions on the use of the one-time repair limit contained in Table 8-2 of this Manual.

5.   Equipment downtime is the time that equipment is not available for use because of CM or SM. It includes all time accrued between the removal of equipment from service and notification to the user that the equipment is ready to return to service. The equipment downtime standard is based on an 8-hour day/240-day year unless the vehicle is used on a 24-hour basis. The maximum Marine Corps acceptable downtime is 10 percent of the total equipment miles (or hours) that the equipment fleet could be available.

6.   GME fleet managers will perform safety inspections, load tests, and calibration procedures for equipment per the instructions in Chapter 9 of this Manual.

7004.   MODIFICATIONS

1.   Normally, GME fleet managers will not modify GME assets. They will establish adequate controls to limit equipment modifications to those required for safety, security, or

accomplishment of the military mission. They may perform limited modifications for such purposes as providing wrecker service or two-way radio service, and for installation of emergency warning devices or auxiliary fire fighting equipment, but only after due consideration of the cost-effectiveness of the action.

2. With the exception of fire fighting apparatus (FFA) and crash fire rescue (CFR) equipment, GME fleet managers may modify, modernize, or alter GME assets without prior approval of HQMC as long as the equipment code does not change as a result of the modification. These types of modifications do not require any record entries other than the SRO.

3. GME fleet managers will submit requests for approval of modifications to FFA and CFR equipment and modifications that necessitate an equipment code change to the CMC (LFS-2). Each request will include justification, vehicle description, Marine Corps registration number, and the estimated cost.

7005. <u>WARRANTIES</u>

1. <u>General Information</u>. GME fleet managers will familiarize themselves with the general provisions of equipment warranties and the significance of such provisions in reducing maintenance costs, as well as timely correction of possible design deficiencies. They will make maximum use of the manufacturer's warranty during the warranty period.

2. <u>Warranty Correction Procedures</u>. If a deficiency exists on a warranted item of equipment, GME fleet managers will attempt to obtain corrective action from the local franchised dealer. GME fleet managers will not take action to correct deficiencies and expect reimbursement by the contractor, unless authorized in writing by either the contractor or the contract administration officer. Negotiations with local franchised dealers are encouraged. However, if GME fleet managers are unable to reach a solution with local franchised dealers, they will so inform the CMC (LFS-2). Additionally, GME fleet managers will submit a SF 368 Product Quality Deficiency Report (PQDR) to HQMC to report major design deficiencies or unsatisfactory conditions (whether or not they occurred during, or corrected under, warranty provisions).

3. <u>In-House Service Warranties.</u> As an option to having the local franchised dealer perform warranty corrective action, GME fleet managers may choose to negotiate an in-house warranty with the local dealer. This arrangement would permit the GME fleet manager to choose either the local franchised dealer or installation maintenance manager to perform a particular warranty repair without violating the warranty or incurring costs. The

contract between the GME fleet manager and the local franchised dealer should specify the provisions that delineate the details of the in-house warranty.

4. Other Defects

    a. The following are standard warranty provisions contained in current procurement contracts: "The contractor hereby guarantees the vehicle and parts thereof against defective material and workmanship for a period of 1 year from the date of acceptance or 12,000 miles road travel, whichever may occur first."

    b. The specified number of miles or years stated in the warranty does not necessarily limit a contractor's responsibility for defective material or workmanship. GME fleet managers will report to the CMC (LFS-2) any abnormal malfunctions or high incident of unusual parts' failures detected at any point beyond the warranty period, if such malfunctions or failures resulted from latent defects and not normal wear and tear. Reports will include a full description and data.

    c. GME fleet managers will expeditiously report safety defects to the CMC (LFS-2). Such notification will include the phrase, "DEFECT WHICH MAY AFFECT SAFETY." The CMC (LFS-2) will provide copies of the defect notification to the activity responsible for leasing the defective equipment, and will coordinate notification of the National Highway Traffic Safety Administration.

7006. RESTRICTIONS ON PRIVATELY-OWNED VEHICLES. GME fleet managers will not authorize or permit the repair, servicing, or manufacturing of privately-owned vehicles, vehicle units, parts, accessories, or equipment in any Marine Corps maintenance facility. Further, they will not authorize or allow the use of government-owned vehicles, tools, motorized equipment, or supplies to service or repair such private property, except when life threatening or emergency conditions occur calling for humanitarian response. No individual may park, garage, or store privately-owned vehicles in any Marine Corps motor pool, shop, or in any building that stores Marine Corps property. The above does not apply to authorized hobby shops.

7007. SUPPLY SUPPORT FOR GME MAINTENANCE

1. Given that reduced downtime is the controlling element of GME maintenance, the GME manager must ensure that adequate supply support is available to complement programmed, productive labor, and associated contract effort.

2. To accomplish this work, MCO 5200.25 provides the activity commander with the general adaptability of obtaining necessary parts, other supplies, tools, and equipment to achieve the most advantageous combination of cost, quality, and responsiveness.

3. Installation commanders should consider using open purchase by means of Indefinite Delivery/Quantity Type Contracts (ID/QTC), Blanket Purchase Agreements (BPA), and Individual Requisitions (IR) for obtaining needed supplies, when there is no mandatory use of specific schedules (e.g., tires, motors, and generators). Such use of open purchase will be in conformance with applicable acquisition regulations (FAR, DoD FAR Supplement, and NAR Supplement) and practiced as specified by the activity Purchasing and Contracting Officer (P&CO).

4. Classes of GME Material Stock. It should not be the intent of the GME fleet manager to establish voluminous stocks of supporting materials and supplies when to do so creates an indefensible burden of inventory management and property accountability. GME fleet managers are advised that it would be more suitable to have the P&CO establish ID/QTC and BPA contracts with locally available commercial vendors who could provide necessary supplies in reasonably responsive times. For purposes of efficient and cost-effective GME maintenance management, the GME manager may establish the following limited stocks to accommodate recurring requirements:

    a. Pre-Expended Bin (PEB). The PEB items are relatively low-cost, fast moving, expendable items designed to facilitate the maintenance function by making everyday use items readily available at the maintenance site, thereby improving productivity of the maintenance technician and reducing equipment downtime. MCO P4790.2 requires GME fleet managers to formulate an internal control and accounting system for the management of PEB. The following PEB stockage criteria apply:

        (1) Unit Price Criteria. These criteria are based on the unit of issue (U/I) and the standard unit price (SUP) of the PEB item. PEB's may include items with a U/I of "pair" or "each", provided the SUP does not exceed $75. For items with other than a U/I of "pair" or "each," the SUP must be $100 or less.

        (2) Usage Criteria. There are no specified PEB usage criteria for GME maintenance, but periodic reviews should eliminate stockage items without sufficient use history.

        (3) Stockage Level Criteria. The quantity of PEB items authorized for stockage will depend on historical usage data available to the GME manager. As a rule, and taking into account the earlier caution against amassing voluminous quantities of materials, stockage levels should contain only sufficient

quantities that would support ready availability criteria and the inability to obtain replenishment from other sources.

    b. <u>Special Operating Stocks (SOS)</u>. The SOS includes items with a value exceeding the established PEB criteria. When deciding to retain a given part or item as SOS, GME fleet managers should consider experience, any history of delays in obtaining the part or item, and any adverse impact such delay has on productivity and reduction in downtime. Annually, the GME fleet manager will review the SOS inventory and certify that items and quantities contained in the inventory are essential to efficient and cost-effective GME maintenance management.

5. <u>Tool Control</u>. GME fleet managers are responsible for establishing inventory management, maintaining internal control, and initiating replacement action for missing or unserviceable tools per appendix D of MCO P4790.2B. It is imperative that GME fleet managers budget for tool replacements to eliminate a shortage of funds when replacing critical tools.

6. <u>Calibration</u>. GME fleet managers are responsible for maintaining a calibration program incorporating the management features of the program described in appendix D of MCO P4790.2B. The program may be manual or automated. GME fleet managers will calibrate all test, measurement, and diagnostic equipment (TMDE) per manufacturer prescribed intervals. If no intervals exist, calibration will be per appendix D of MCO P4790.2B. The GME fleet manager will select the calibration service source.

7008. <u>PUBLICATIONS</u>. Each GME fleet manager will establish a publication control system per appendix B of MCO P4790.2B.

7009. <u>ANTIFREEZE INSTRUCTIONS</u>. GME fleet managers will add antifreeze to GME per manufacturer's recommendations to maintain thermal protection suitable for the location in which the equipment operates.

7010. <u>TIRES</u>. GE fleet managers may use reconditioned (regrooved, retread, or recapped) tires as replacement tires on GME, including trailers, with the following exceptions:

1. No bus shall operate with reconditioned tires on the front (steering) axle.

2. No truck or truck tractor shall operate with regrooved tires on the front (steering) axle that has a load carrying capacity equal to or greater than that of 8.25-20 8 ply-rating tires.

3. GME fleet managers will use only reconditioned tires procured or renewed from sources that meet standards promulgated in 49 Code of Federal Regulations.

Legend for Marking

A - Adjust   S - Service   X - Adjustment/Repair Required
C - Check   V - Verify   O - Defect Correct
L - Lubricate / - Not Applicable

NO.	COVERAGE	BEFORE	DURING	AFTER	8-Hr	10-Hr
1	DAMAGE, PILFERAGE LOSS	C		C		
2	LEAKS, GENERAL	C		C		
3	FUEL, OIL, WATER	V		S		
4	ENGINE WARMUP	C				
5	INSTRUMENTS	C	C			
6	SAFETY DEVICES	C				
7	TOOLS AND EQUIPMENT	C				
8	PUBLICATIONS	V				
9	CLUTCH	V	C			
10	STEERING	C	C			
11	ENGINE OPERATION		C			
12	UNUSUAL NOISES	C	C			
13	LIGHTS AND REFLECTORS	C				
14	AIR TANKS	S		S		
15	DRIVE BELTS	C		C		
16	BATTERY ELEC. LEVEL	C		S		
17	ANTIFREEZE TEST TO F	V				
18	SERVICE BRAKES	V	C			
19	TRANSMISSION	C	C			
20	AIR FILTER	V		S		
21	FUEL FILTERS	S		S		
22	TIRES/TRACK	C		C		
23	CLEANLINESS	C		V		
24						
25						
26						
27						
28						
29						
30						

    NOTE: Add other procedures designated by the
            appropriate service manual.

REMARKS

Figure 7-1.--Operator's Service Checklist.

GARRISON MOBILE EQUIPMENT

CHAPTER 8

INVENTORY MANAGEMENT

FIGURE

TABLE

GARRISON MOBILE EQUIPMENT

CHAPTER 8

INVENTORY MANAGEMENT

8000. GENERAL INFORMATION

1. The CMC (LFS-2) manages the centralized Garrison Mobile Equipment Inventory Management System (GME-MS). The GME-MS contains a file of pertinent information for all active GME equipment and is used to track GME fleet acquisitions, use, transfer, and disposal. It is imperative that GME fleet managers update their fleet within GME-MS after every change to their inventory.

2. The CMC (LFS-2) will assign a G-TAM control number (equipment code) for each item of GME. The G-TAM control number describes allowances and categorizes the budget. Table 8-1 contains a description of each of the equipment codes.

3. GME fleet managers will manage the inventory of all GME charged to their account, including that procured or leased by either appropriated or non-appropriated funds.

4. T/E allowances and projected retirement years, as described in chapter 3 of this Manual, will generate equipment procurement schedules for appropriated funded vehicles.

5. Upon receipt of instructions from the CMC (LFS-2), GME fleet managers will properly dispose of any equipment that meets prescribed criteria for disposal.

6. Wherever practical, GME fleet managers may submit reports required by this chapter by automated electronic means using the reports contained in this chapter, or other similar reports conveying the same data. Coordinate with the CMC (LFS-2) prior to submitting non-standard reports.

8001. GME FILE MAINTENANCE

1. GME fleet managers will report receiving an item of GME to the CMC (LFS-2) by forwarding a copy of DD Form 1342 (DoD Property Record) annotated with the equipment code and USMC registration number. Automated reporting procedures are efficient and encouraged.

2. Throughout the life of the equipment, GME fleet managers will update the GME-MS file as necessary using the format shown in Figure 8-1. Updates need include only the registration number and the appropriate changes to the particular information field.

3. GME fleet managers will report the annual usage data for all GME (except trailers) to the CMC (LFS-2) utilizing the Activity Utilization Report contained in TM-4700-15/1 or a similar locally produced report.

4. The following utilization codes apply for GME:

Code	Description
CA	Class A assignment
CB	Class B assignment
CC	Class C pool assignment
WD	Awaiting disposal
SP	Special purpose equipment

8002. EQUIPMENT RECEIPT AND DISPOSAL PROCEDURES

1. Equipment is eligible for disposal when it meets one of the following criteria:

    a. Exceeds life expectancy in years (table 8-1).

    b. Exceeds life expectancy in usage (table 8-1).

    c. Exceeds one-time repair limit (table 8-2).

    d. Exceeds T/E allowance.

2. Equipment With Excessive Years or Usage. When an item of equipment exceeds either the life expectancy in years or in usage as contained in table 8-1, GME fleet managers may properly dispose of the item and within 15 days report the disposal to the CMC (LFS-2). GME fleet managers need not request authorization prior to disposal.

3. Equipment Exceeds One-time Repair Limit or T/E. When an item of equipment exceeds the one-time repair limit contained in table 8-2, GME fleet managers will request disposal instructions from the CMC (LFS-2). The request will consist of a limited technical inspection (LTI) with a cover letter. GME fleet managers will obtain disposal authorization prior to disposal of equipment.

4. Serviceable Equipment - Requesting Retention. If an item of equipment meets one of the preceding criteria listed in paragraph 8002.1, but still is in serviceable condition and the GME fleet

manager desires to retain the equipment, the letter requesting a waiver of disposal instructions should so indicate. While awaiting instructions, GME fleet managers may continue to operate and maintain the equipment.

5. Serviceable - Requesting Transfer. If an item of equipment meets one of the preceding criteria listed in paragraph 8002.1 but still is in serviceable condition and another activity has need of it, the letter requesting disposal instructions should so indicate. While awaiting instructions, GME fleet managers may transfer the equipment on a temporary loan basis.

6. The following actions apply when delivering GME to a Defense Reutilization and Marketing Office:

    a. The CMC (LFS-2) will change the utilization code of the item to awaiting disposal (WD) and enter the WD code in the GME-MS file (example: WD CMC Disp Ltr 4500/8 26 Sep 98). This will ensure the equipment no longer counts against an activity's allowances.

    b. Before delivering equipment to DRMO, GME fleet managers will remove or deface Marine Corps identification markings as required by NavCompt Manual, volume III.

    c. Within 15 days of disposal, GME fleet managers will send a completed copy of DD Form 1348-1 (DoD Single Line Item Release/Receipt Document) to the CMC (LFS-2) to report compliance with instructions and to have the item deleted from the GME-MS file.

7. Upon receipt of new equipment, GME fleet managers will enter appropriate data in the GME-MS file and within 15 days send DD Form 1342 (DoD Property Record) to the CMC (LFS-2).

8. The responsibility for forwarding DD Forms 1342 and 1348-1 rests with the GME fleet manager.

8003. ONE-TIME REPAIR LIMIT

1. If an item of equipment requires extensive repairs, GME fleet managers will conduct an LTI to determine if it is economical to repair the item. Table 8-2 contains the one-time repair limits.

2. Should the repair estimate exceed the one-time repair limit, GME fleet managers will request either disposal instructions or a waiver of the limit from the CMC (LFS-2). The request will include only a completed LTI and cover letter. In the case of a request for a waiver, the cover letter will contain necessary justification.

3. Because the status of replacement items is the chief concern in approving waivers of the one-time repair limit and local procurement provides almost all GME for MCAS, Iwakuni, and MCB, Camp Butler, the commanders of those activities may waive the one-time repair limit.

8004. TRANSFER OF EQUIPMENT

1. GME fleet managers will request authority from the CMC (LFS-2) prior to transferring equipment from their activity to another. They will forward a copy of the request to the gaining activity. The CMC (LFS-2) will return the approved transfer to the losing activity with a copy to the gaining activity.

2. Upon approving the transfer, HQMC will update the GME-MS file so no further reporting of the transaction is necessary by the GME fleet managers.

3. While awaiting formal approval of the transfer, the GME fleet managers may transfer the equipment on a temporary loan basis.

8005. MANUFACTURER CODE

1. Table 8-3, Manufacturer Codes, contains codes necessary to maintain and update the GME-MS.

8006. AGENCY REPORT OF MOTOR VEHICLE DATA

1. GME fleet managers will measure the effectiveness of equipment activities under their control during the previous fiscal year. Using either paper or electronic means, they will prepare and submit the SF-82 Agency Report of Motor Vehicle Data to the CMC (LFS-2) by the first week of November. Figure 8-2 shows a sample report (Report Control Symbol DD-11240-01). Fleet managers may find an electronic copy of the SF-82 available at: http://policyworks.gov/org/main/mt/homepage/mtv/sf82.pdf Instructions for the preparation of this report include:

    a. Reportable Vehicles. Reportable vehicles will include non-tactical motor vehicles such as sedans, station wagons, carryalls, vans, ambulances, buses, trucks, and truck tractors. The following vehicles are exempt from the report:

        (1) Trailers and trailing equipment regardless of type or size.

        (2) Trucks with permanently mounted equipment.

(3) Air compressors.

(4) Motorcycles.

(5) Military design (tactical) vehicles, including those temporarily assigned as GME assets.

(6) Special purpose vehicles (such as fire, wrecker, maintenance, refuse, high lift, oil, fuel, and industrial tractors).

(7) Construction and installation maintenance equipment (such as cranes, dump trucks, snowplows, sweepers, loaders, and graders).

(8) Material handling equipment.

(9) Scooters (2-, 3-, or 4-wheel -- all classes).

(10) GSA vehicles.

(11) Vehicles provided by contractors.

b. <u>Title line</u>. GME fleet managers will submit separate forms for domestic and foreign based vehicles. Place an (x) in the Vehicles Based block indicating whether the report reflects domestic or foreign vehicles. Other entries are self-explanatory. Domestic vehicles include those located in the 50 States, the Territories, the Commonwealth of Puerto Rico, and the District of Columbia.

c. Complete sections I, II, and III, using the reporting procedures on the back of the SF 82.

d. Complete section IV, parts A, B, and C - Total Vehicles Owned and Leased. This section is for DOE energy reporting requirements. List in part A, B, or C, by fuel type, the total number of vehicles on hand as of September 30. Use the following instructions to determine the specific date to be shown in each part of this section:

(1) Section IV, part A: Agency-Owned and Commercially Leased Vehicles. Total Fleet vehicles, by fuel type, on hand. The number of vehicles reported here should be the same as reported in section I, Agency-Owned and Leased vehicles for all vehicles on hand for the fiscal year ending September 30. Do not include GSA IFMS provided vehicles.

      (2)   Section IV, part B: Acquisitions This Year. List by fuel type, all vehicles acquired this fiscal year. Include purchased, converted, and commercially leased (long-term).

     NOTE: A flexible fuel or bi-fuel vehicle should not be shown only in the appropriate alternative fuel column, and not also shown in the gasoline column. For example, a vehicle capable of operating on either E85 or gasoline would only be shown in the ethanol column; similarly, a vehicle capable of operating on natural gas (NG) or gasoline would only be shown in the NG column.

      (3)   Section IV, part C. Annual Fuel Consumption Report By Fuel Type. Include total fuel consumed by fuel type for all vehicles on hand for the fiscal year ending September 30. Do not include GSA IFMS provided vehicles. The major fuel types are listed, including alternative fuels. Include owned, and commercially leased (long-term) vehicle fuel consumption. For alternative fuels (anything other than pure gasoline or diesel), convert the fuel used to gasoline equivalent gallons (GEG's) using the Fuel Conversion Ratio Table shown on the SF-82. If other fuels are used, develop a GEG factor by dividing the heat content of the fuel in Btu's (higher heating value) by the heat content of a gallon of gasoline (125,000 Btu's for the value of a gallon of gasoline.)

```
_____6)      (G)_____(4)        _____(6)      _____(4)
Registration    Equip. Code          Equip. Loc.      Mfg. Yr.
Number          (G-TAM CN)           (T/E No.)


_____(4)     _____(6)    _____(5)      _____(6)
Ret. Yr.        Procurement          FY MI/HR         Total MI/HR
                Cost                 (Last FY)
                (Dollars Only)


_____(8)     _____(3)    _____(9)
PWO Number            Mfg. Code            Chassis Serial No.
                                           (HQMC entry)


_____(2)          _____(30)
Utilization Code           Remarks Code


_____(10)
Future Use
```

NOTE: Numbers in parentheses indicate the maximum
       number of alpha/numeric characters in that
       field.

Figure 8-1.--GME-MS File Format.

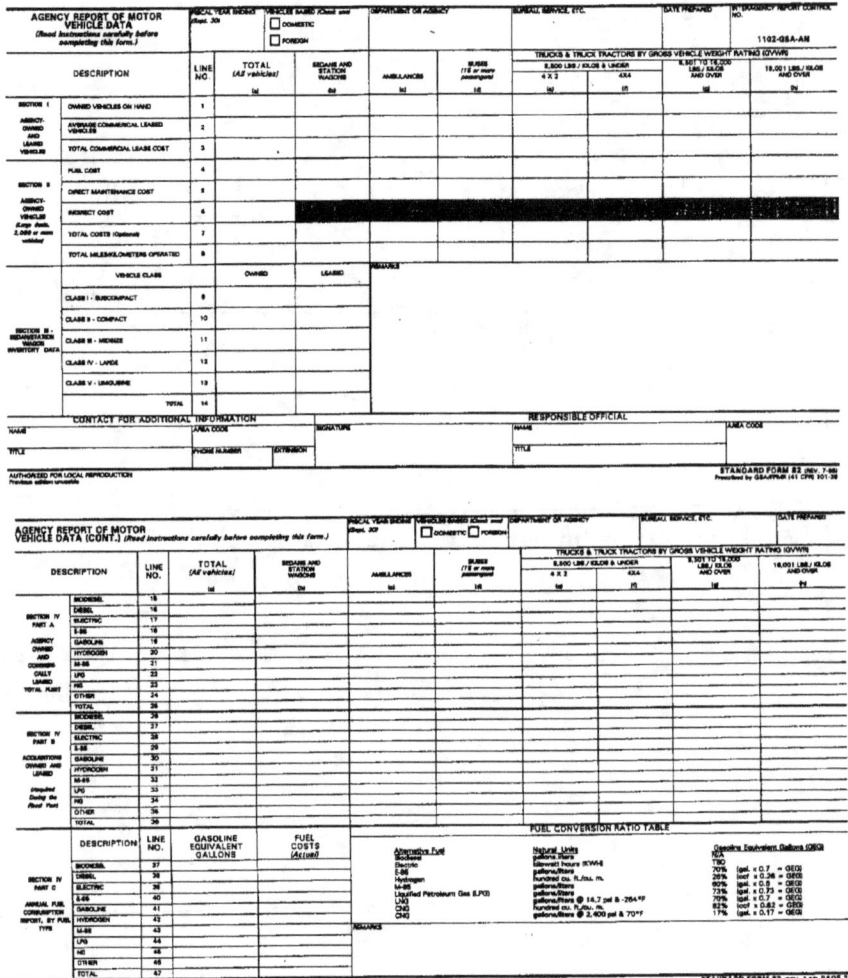

Figure 8-2.--Agency Report of Motor Vehicle Data.

GARRISON MOBILE EQUIPMENT

Table 8-1.--GME Codes.

Equip Code	DoD Group	Description	Life Expectancy Years	Miles
G0100	F	Ambulance, Commercial	7	84,000
G0101	B	Bus, school, 28-passenger	8	84,000
G0102	D	Bus, school, 36-passenger	8	84,000
G0103	B	Bus, school, 20-passenger	8	84,000
G0104	D	Bus, inter-city	12	280,000
G0105	C	Bus, school, 44-pass	10	150,000
G0106	B	Bus, adult, 20-pass	8	84,000
G0107	B	Bus, adult, 28-pass	8	84,000
G0108	D	Bus, adult, 36-pass	8	84,000
G0110	C	Bus, adult, 44-pass	10	150,000
G0202	C	Vehicle Troop Trans	10	150,000
G0303	A	Sedan, compact	3	60,000
G0305	A	Sedan, law enforcement	3	60,000
G0402	E	Station Wagon, compact	3	60,000
G0500	H	Utility Vehicle, 4x4	6	72,000
G0501	H	Van, 8-passenger	6	72,000
G0502	H	Van, wagon, compact, 5-7 passenger	6	72,000
G0503	H	Van, cargo, compact	6	72,000
G0504	O	Van, maint, compact	6	72,000
G0505	O	Utility vehicle, 4x2	6	72,000
G0508	G	Pickup, compact, 4x2	6	72,000
G0509	G	Pickup, compact, 4x4	6	72,000

Table 8-1.--GME Codes--Continued.

Equip Code	DoD Group	Description	Life Expectancy Years	Miles
G0510	H	Truck, gen maint, compact	6	72,000
G0544		TAC-AIK Util vehicle, 4x4		
G0555		SWA vehicle-AIK		
G0601	G	Pickup, 1/2-T, 4x2	6	72,000
G0603	O	Truck, gen maint, 1/2-T	6	72,000
G0604	G	Pickup, 1/2-T, 4x4	6	72,000
G0605	O	Step van	7	72,000
G0606	H	Carryall, 4x2	6	72,000
G0607	H	Truck, stake, 1/2-T	6	72,000
G0608	H	Carryall, 4x4	6	72,000
G0701	H	Pickup, 3/4-T, 4 dr	6	72,000
G0715	H	Van, law enf, 3/4-T	6	72,000
G0802	O	Truck, general maint, 1-T, 4x4	7	84,000
G0803	O	Truck, general maint, 1-T, 4x4	7	84,000
G0804	O	Truck, aerial boom, 1-T	7	84,000
G0805	I	Pickup, 1-T, 4x4	7	84,000
G0806	H	Truck, multistop, 1-T	7	84,000
G0808	I	Carrier, tracked, pers	7	84,000
G0809	I	Carrier, tracked, cargo	7	84,000
G0810	H	Van, cargo, 1-T	7	84,000
G0811	I	Truck, stake, 1-T	7	84,000

Table 8-1.--GME Codes--Continued.

Equip Code	DoD Group	Description	Life Expectancy Years	Miles
G0812	O	Wrecker, 1-T, 4x2	7	84,000
G0817	I	Pickup, 1-T, 4-dr, crewcab	7	84,000
G0825	H	Van, 15-passenger	7	84,000
G0888		AIK, CUCV, 1 1/4 T, 4x4		
G0900	H	Hummer, Commercial	7	84,000
G0901	O	Truck, line maint, 1 1/2-T	7	84,000
G0902	J	Truck, multi-stop, 1 1/2-T	7	84,000
G0904	J	Truck, stake, 1 1/2-T	7	84,000
G0905	J	Truck, stake, 1 1/2-T, 4x4	7	84,000
G0922	J	Truck, dump, 2-T	7	84,000
G0923	J	Truck, stake, 2-T	7	84,000
G0924	J	Truck, van, 2-T	7	84,000
G0925	J	Truck, refrigerator, 2-T	7	84,000
G1101	L	Truck, cargo, 3-T	8	84,000
G1102	L	Truck, van, 3-T	8	84,000
G1104	O	Truck, line maint, 3-T	8	84,000
G1106	L	Truck, stake, 3-T	8	84,000
G1116	O	Truck, aerial boom, 3-T	8	84,000
G1118	O	Truck, refrigerator, 3-T	8	84,000
G1124	O	Truck, line maint, 3-T, 4x4	8	84,000

GARRISON MOBILE EQUIPMENT

Table 8-1.--GME Codes--Continued.

Equip Code	DoD Group	Description	Life Expectancy Years	Miles
G1125	O	Truck, lubrication, 3-T, 4x4	8	84,000
G1128	L	Truck, cargo, 3-T, 4x4	8	84,000
G1130	O	Truck, 3-T, hydraulic lift body	8	84,000
G1201	M	Truck, dump, 5-T	10	150,000
G1202	M	Truck, tractor, 5-T	10	150,000
G1204	O	Truck, garbage, 5-T	10	150,000
G1130	O	Truck, 3-T, hydraulic lift body	8	84,000
G1201	M	Truck, dump, 5-T	10	150,000
G1202	M	Truck, tractor, 5-T	10	150,000
G1204	O	Truck, garbage, 5-T	10	150,000
G1205	O	Truck, line maint, 5-T	10	150,000
G1206	O	Truck, dumpster, 5-T	10	150,000
G1208	M	Truck, tractor, 5-T, 6x4	10	150,000
G1209	O	Truck, aerial boom, 5-T	10	150,000
G1210	M	Truck, tractor, 5-T, 6x6	10	150,000
G1211	O	Wrecker, 5-T, 4x2	10	150,000
G1212	O	Wrecker, 5-T, 6x4	10	150,000
G1214	O	Truck, sewer maint, 5-T	10	150,000
G1215	O	Truck, aerial boom, 5-T, 6x4	10	150,000
G1216	O	Truck, dump, 5-T, 4x4	10	150,000

Table 8-1.--GME Codes--Continued.

Equip Code	DoD Group	Description	Life Expectancy Years	Miles
G1217	O	Truck, line maint, 5-T, 4x4	10	150,000
G1222	M	Truck, Tractor, 5-T, 6x6	10	150,000
G1223	M	Truck, van, 5-T	10	150,000
G1226	M	Truck, dump, 5-T, 6x4	10	150,000
G1227	M	Truck, stake, 5-T, 6x4	10	150,000
G1228	M	Truck, stake, 5-T	10	150,000
G1301	M	Truck, dump, 10-T, 6x4	10	150,000
G1302	M	Truck, tractor, 7 1/2-T	10	150,000
G1304	M	Truck, tractor, 15-T, 6x4	12	300,000
G1306	M	Truck, tractor, 10-T, 6x4	10	150,000
G1307	O	Truck, dumpmaster, 10-T, 6x4	10	150,000
G1308	O	Wrecker, 10-T, 6x6	10	150,000
G1309	O	Truck, 10-T, equipment transportation/crane	10	150,000
G1313	O	Truck, 10-T, 6x4	10	150,000
G1315	O	Truck, line maint, 7-1/2-T, 4x4	10	150,000
G1401	O	Truck, tank, 1,000 gal	8	84,000
G1402	O	Truck, tank, 2,000 gal	10	150,000
G1403	O	Truck, tank, 1,000 gal, 4x4	8	84,000
G1404	O	Truck, tank, 2,400 gal, 6x4	10	150,000

Table 8-1.--GME Codes--Continued.

Equip Code	DoD Group	Description	Life Expectancy Years	Miles
G1406	O	Truck, tank, 1,200 gal, 4x4	8	84,000
G1407	O	Truck, flusher, 2,000 gal, 6x6	10	150,000
G1408	O	Truck, tank, 2,000 gal, 6x6	10	150,000
G1409	O	Truck, tank, 1,000 gal, 4x4	8	84,000
G1410	O	Truck, flusher, 3,000 gal, 6x4	10	150,000
G1411	O	Truck, tank, LPG, 2,400 gal, 4x2	10	150,000
G1412	O	Truck, tank, 500 gal	8	84,000
G1415	O	Truck, tank, 5,000 gal, 6x4	10	150,000
G1501	X	Truck, fire, Class A pumper	12	300,000
G1502	X	Truck, fire, ladder	15	
G1504	X	Truck, Rescue, P10	10	
G1505	X	Truck, fire, brush, 4x4	12	
G1507	X	Truck, fire, rescue	10	
G1508	X	Truck, mobile TAU	10	
G1510	X	Truck, fire, brush, 6x6	12	
G1511	X	CFR nurse unit	10	
G1513	X	Truck, CFR, P-19	10	
G1514	X	Truck, fire, Water tower	12	
G1515	Y	Crane, CFR, salvage	10	

Table 8-1.--GME Codes--Continued.

Equip Code	DoD Group	Description	Life Expectancy Years	Miles
G1602	P	Trailer, equipment Transporter	15	
G1603	P	Trailer, cargo, 2-wheel	15	
G1604	P	Trailer, Hazardous Material	15	
G1605	P	Trailer, Recycling	15	
G1606	P	Trailer, car hauler	15	
G1607	P	Trailer, water, 2-wheel	15	
G1614	P	Trailer, horse	15	
G1619	P	Trailer, semi, van	15	
G1620	P	Trailer, semi, Refrigeration	15	
G1622	P	Trailer, semi, 12-T	15	
G1623	P	Trailer, semi, 20-T	15	
G1624	P	Trailer, semi, 15-20-T, low bed	15	
G1625	P	Trailer, semi, 25-T, low bed	15	
G1626	P	Trailer, semi, 35-T, low bed	15	
G1629	P	Trailer, semi, 60-T, low bed	15	
G1630	P	Trailer, semi, Tank hauler	15	
G1631	P	Trailer, semi, dump	15	
G1632	P	Trailer, semi, Dump, bottom	15	

GARRISON MOBILE EQUIPMENT

Table 8-1.--GME Codes--Continued.

Equip Code	DoD Group	Description	Life Expectancy Years	Miles
G1633	P	Trailer, semi, tank	15	
G1634	P	Trailer, semi, water	15	
G1640	P	Trailer, mobile power	15	
G1641	P	Dolly converter	15	
G1642	P	Trailer, line maint	15	
G1643	P	Trailer, fiber optic	15	
G1654	P	Trailer, tank, 500 gal	15	
G1657	P	Trailer, semi, Tank, 5,000 gal	15	
G1666	P	Trailer, cargo, 2-wheel	15	
G1677	P	Trailer, water, 2-wheel	15	
G1706	R	Forklift, fuel, 4,000 lbs	8	
G1713	R	Forklift, fuel, 6,000 lbs	8	
G1719	R	Forklift, fuel, 15,000 lbs	10	
G1720	R	Forklift, fuel, 92,500 lbs	15	
G1721	R	Forklift, fuel, 25,000 lbs	15	
G1723	R	Forklift, fuel, 10,000 lbs	10	
G1735	R	Forklift, rough terrain, 6,000 lbs	8	

GARRISON MOBILE EQUIPMENT

Table 8-1.--GME Codes--Continued.

Equip Code	DoD Group	Description	Life Expectancy Years	Miles
G1801	R	Forklift, elec, 2,000 lbs	15	
G1805	R	Forklift, elec, 4,000 lbs	15	
G1806	R	Forklift, elec, 4,000 lbs, narrow aisle	15	
G1807	R	Forklift, elec, 6,000 lbs	15	
G1901	R	Stock selector, fuel, 4,000 lbs	8	
G1903	R	Stock selector, elec, 2,000 lbs	15	
G2002	R	Tractor, whse, fuel, 4,000 lbs, DBP	8	
G2004	R	Tractor, whse, fuel, 7,500 lbs DBP	8	
G2006	R	Tractor, whse, fuel, 10,000 lbs DBP	10	
G2021	R	Transporter, loader	15	
G2204	R	Crane, whse, fuel, 10,000 lbs	12	
G2205	R	Crane, whse, fuel, 20,000 lbs	12	
G2303	R	Straddle truck, fuel	15	
G2400	Z	Scooter, elec, cargo	3	
G2401	Z	Scooter, fuel, cargo	3	
G2402	Z	Scooter, elec, pass	3	
G2409	Z	Scooter, law enforcement, Motorcycle	3	

GARRISON MOBILE EQUIPMENT

Table 8-1.--GME Codes--Continued.

Equip Code	DoD Group	Description	Life Expectancy Years	Miles
G2410	Z	Snowmobile	5	
G2504	R	Pallet truck, elec, Nontiering	15	
G2604	R	Pallet truck, elec, Tiering	15	
G3011	T	Asphalt distributor Attachment	6	
G3012	S	Asphalt finisher	8	
G3013	T	Curb paver	8	
G3020	S	Concrete mixer truck	6	
G3030	S	Asphalt distributor truck	8	
G3032	S	Rock crusher	8	
G3033	S	Paving material spreader	6	
G3034	S	Oil distributor truck	8	
G3037	T	Sander attachment	10	
G3045	T	Asphalt patching trailer	6	
G3046	T	Water distributor	8	
G3047	T	Asphalt heating trailer	12	
G3060	T	Asphalt mixer	8	
G3100	S	Compressor, air, 60-104 CFM	6	
G3110	S	Compressor, air, 105-125 CFM	6	
G3112	S	Compressor, air, 126-250 CFM	8	

GARRISON MOBILE EQUIPMENT

Table 8-1.--GME Codes--Continued.

Equip Code	DoD Group	Description	Life Expectancy Years	Miles
G3113	S	Compressor, air, 251-500 CFM	8	
G3126	S	Platform, hydraulic	15	
G3131	S	Crane, crawler, 10-T	10	
G3134	S	Crane, crawler, 150-T	12	
G3150	S	Ditching machine	7	
G3160	S	Excavator, multipurpose	10	
G3165	S	Road grader	8	
G3168	S	Belt loader	7	
G3170	S	Scoop loader, tracked	7	
G3171	S	Scoop loader, wheeled,	7	
G3177	S	Scoop loader, wheeled, 5-yd3	7	
G3178	S	Scoop loader, mini	7	
G3181	T	Roller, wobble wheel	8	
G3183	T	Roller, vibrating	6	
G3185	S	Roller, 3-wheel	10	
G3187	T	Roller, sheepsfoot	10	
G3188	S	Roller, tandem	10	
G3192	N	Dump truck, off-road	8	
G3197	T	Scraper, self-propelled	7	
G3210	S	Bulldozer, 105 flywheel Hp	9	
G3220	S	Bulldozer, 140 flywheel Hp	9	

Table 8-1.--GME Codes--Continued.

Equip Code	DoD Group	Description	Life Expectancy Years	Miles
G3225	S	Bulldozer, 195 flywheel Hp	9	
G3230	S	Bulldozer, 300 flywheel Hp	9	
G3240	T	Tractor, armored, Range maintenance	15	
G3250	S	Compactor, land fill	6	
G3300	T	Floodlight	8	
G3301	T	Voltage test trailer	10	
G3409	S	Blower, trailer, leaf	6	
G3410	S	Sweeper, runway	6	
G3412	S	Cleaner, sewer, Trailer	6	
G3413	S	Cleaner, Vacuum, dump	6	
G3414	S	Cleaner, catch basin	6	
G3415	S	Cleaner, septic tank	6	
G3417	S	Cleaner, Hazardous Waste	6	
G3418	S	Cleaner, Recycling	6	
G3430	T	Marker, traffic line	6	
G3450	Z	Water purification Unit	15	
G3490	T	Mower, gang, tractor	6	
G3502	T	Stump cutter	6	
G3506	T	Brush shredder	6	
G3509	T	Tree spade	6	

Table 8-1.--GME Codes--Continued.

Equip Code	DoD Group	Description	Life Expectancy Years	Miles
G3600	S	Tractor, garden	5	
G3610	U	Tractor, agriculture, 30 DBH	6	
G3630	U	Tractor, automotive	6	
G3640	U	Tractor, agriculture, 50 DBH	6	
G3650	U	Tractor, industrial, 50 DBH	6	
G3651	U	Tractor, industrial, 70 DBH	6	
G3660	U	Tractor, industrial, Loader/backhoe	6	
G3670	U	Tractor, industrial, Over 160 DBH	7	
G3700	T	Sweeper, warehouse	4	
G3701	S	Sweeper, street	7	
G3702	S	Sweeper, magnet	7	
G3720	T	Snowplow	7	
G3800	V	Railway car, flat	28	
G3801	W	Railway car, maint	15	
G3804	W	Railway locomotive	25	
G3007	W	Trackmobile	15	
G3808	W	Electromatic, tamper	15	
G3901	Y	Crane, truck mounted, 2-engine, 5-20-T	10	
G3902	Y	Crane, truck mounted, 2-engine, 21-35-T	10	

Table 8-1.--GME Codes--Continued.

Equip Code	DoD Group	Description	Life Expectancy Years	Miles
G3903	Y	Crane, truck mounted, 2-engine, over 35-T	10	
G3908	Y	Crane, straddle	N/A	
G3909	Y	Crane, truck mounted, Hydraulic, 31-40-T	10	
G3910	Y	Crane, truck mounted, Hydraulic, 20-30-T	10	
G3911	Y	Crane, CRF, salvage	10	
G3913	Y	Knuckle boom truck	10	
G3915	Y	Materials handler, Boom	10	

GME VLP Codes
Code Description

Code	Description
G4101	BUS (GSA-3220), SCHOOL 24/28-PAX
G4102	BUS (GSA-3222), SCHOOL 36-PAX
G4103	BUS (GSA-3218), SCHOOL 16/20-PAX
G4104	BUS (GSA-3290/3292), INTERCITY
G4105	BUS (GSA-3224), SCHOOL 44-PAX
G4106	BUS (GSA-3240), ADULT 20-PAX
G4107	BUS (GSA-3242), ADULT 28-PAX
G4108	BUS (GSA-3244), ADULT 36-PAX
G4110	BUS (GSA-3246), ADULT 44-PAX
G4303	SEDAN (GSA-1200), COMPACT
G4305	SEDAN (GSA-1125), LAW-PATROL, MIDSIZE
G4500	UTILITY VEHICLE (GSA-6100), 4x4
G4501	VAN (GSA-4215), 8-PAX, 3/4-T, 4x2
G4502	VAN (GSA-4115), COMPACT, 7-PAX, 1/2-T, 4x2
G4503	VAN (GSA-4110), CARGO, COMPACT, 1/2-T
G4504	VAN (GSA-4113), MAINT, COMPACT
G4505	UTILITY VEHICLE (GSA-4100), 4x2
G4508	PICKUP (GSA-4150), COMPACT, 1/2-T, 4x2
G4509	PICKUP (GSA-6150), COMPACT, 1/2-T, 4x4
G4510	TRUCK (GSA-4255), GEN MAINT, 1/2-T
G4601	PICKUP (GSA-4250), 3/4-T, 4x2
G4603	TRUCK (GSA-4255), GEN MAINT, 3/4-T

Table 8-1.--GME Codes--Continued.

```
GME VLP Codes
Code   Description

G4604   PICKUP (GSA-6250), 3/4-T, 4x4
G4605   STEP VAN (GSA-4266)
G4606   CARRYALL (GSA-4375), 1 1/2-T, 4x2
G4608   CARRYALL (GSA-6375), 1 1/2-T, 4x4
G4701   PICKUP (GSA-4252), CREW CAB
G4715   VAN (GSA-4310), CARGO LAW ENF, 1 1/2-T
G4803   TRUCK (GSA-4355), GEN MAINT, 1 1/4-T
G4805   PICKUP (GSA-6350), 1 1/2-T, 4x4
G4806   STEP VAN (GSA-4366), 1-T
G4810   VAN (GSA-4310), CARGO, 1 1/2-T
G4811   TRUCK (GSA-4280), STAKE, 1 1/4-T, 4x2
G4817   PICKUP (GSA-4352), Crew Cab, 1 1/2-T, 4x2
G4825   VAN (GSA-4315), 15-PAX, 1 1/2-T, 4x2
G4902   TRUCK (GSA-4366), VAN MULTISTOP, 1 1/2-T
G4904   TRUCK (GSA-4380), STAKE, 1 3/4-T

GSA Leased Codes
Code   Description

G5192   Bus, school, 36-passenger
G5193   Bus, school, 20-passenger
G5194   Bus, intercity
G5199   Bus, school, 60-passenger
G5393   Sedan, Compact
G5395   Sedan, Compact, patrol
G5396   Sedan, Mid-Sized
G5492   Station Wagon, compact
G5590   Utility vehicle
G5591   Van, 8-passenger
G5598   Pickup, compact
G5690   Stepvan
G5691   Pickup, 1/2-T, 4x2
G5694   Pickup 1/2-T, 4x4
G5698   Carryall
G5890   Van, 1-T
G5892   Van, 15-pass
C5896   Truck, multistop


Commercial Lease Codes
Code   Description

G6192   Bus, school, 36-passenger
G6193   Bus, school, 20-passenger
G6194   Bus, intercity
```

Table 8-1.--GME Codes--Continued.

```
Commercial Lease Codes
Code    Description

G6199   Bus, school, 60-passenger
G6393   Sedan, Compact
G6395   Sedan, Compact, patrol
G6396   Sedan, Mid-Sized
G6492   Station Wagon, compact
G6590   Utility vehicle
G6591   Van, 8-passenger
G6598   Pickup, compact
G6690   Stepvan
G6691   Pickup, 1/2-T, 4x2
G6694   Pickup 1/2-T, 4x4
G6698   Carryall
G6890   Van, 1-T
G6892   Van, 15-pass
G6896   Truck, multistop
```

Table 8-2.-- Factors for Use in Equipment One-Time Repair
Determinations.

Current Age of Equipment

Life Exp In Yrs	1	2	3	4	5	6	7	8	9	10	11	12	13	14	15	16	17	18	19 to 25
3	36	23	10																
4	40	30	20	10															
5	42	34	26	18	10														
6	43	36	30	23	16	10													
7	43	38	33	27	21	15	10												
8	45	40	35	30	25	20	15	10											
9	45	41	36	32	28	23	19	14	10										
10	46	42	38	34	30	26	22	18	14	10									
11	46	42	39	36	33	28	24	22	17	13	10								
12	46	43	40	38	36	30	26	23	20	16	13	10							
15	47	44	42	39	36	34	31	28	26	23	20	18	15	12	10				
25	48	47	45	44	42	40	39	37	36	34	32	31	29	28	26	24	23	21	20

NOTE: The one-time repair limit is determined by finding the life expectancy in years for the Equipment Code of the equipment under consideration. Then go to the column showing the current age of the equipment. Multiply the factor (expressed as a percentage or decimal) obtained by the original acquisition cost of the equipment.

Table 8-3.--Manufacturer Codes.

Code	Manufacturer
ABM	AFC Brill Motors Corporation
ABS	Abbe-Schmidt, Inc.
ACC	American Colemen Company
ACO	Anthony Company
ADW	Adams Division of Letournean Westinghouse
AHD	American Hoist and Derrick Company
ALC	Allis Chalmers
AMC	American Motors Corporation
AMF	Atlantic Manufacturing Company
AMG	AM General Corporation
APC	Athey Products Corporation
API	Aeroil Products Company, Incorporated
ARI	Ariens Company
ARI	ARPS Corporation (Subsidiary of Chromalloy Corp.)
ART	Artic Cat
ASC	Asplundh Chipper Company
ATE	American Tractor Equipment Corporation
AUS	Austin Products, Incorporated
AUT	Automatic Transportation Company
AWC	Austin Western Company
BAL	Barnard and Leas Manufacturing Company, Inc.
BAY	Bay City, Incorporated
BCR	Besler Corporation
BEC	Bucyrus-Erie Company
BEN	Bendi Corp.
BES	Best Trailer Corp.
BGC	Barber Green Company
BJM	Big Joe Manufacturing Company
BLM	Baker-Lull Manufacturing Company
BLU	Blue Bird Buses, Inc.
BMD	Buick Motors Division
BNC	Beaver National Coach Manufacturing Company
BOB	Bobcat, Inc.
BOU	Boughman Manufacturing Company
BRA	Branham, Inc.
BRL	Baker Raulang
BRY	Burry Corporation
BSM	Box Shrader Magnetic Products
BTA	Buffalo Turbine Agricultural Equipment Company
BTC	Brown Tank Company
BUC	Buck Equipment Company
BWI	Bob Wilson, Incorporated

Table 8-3.--Manufacturer Codes--Continued.

Code	Manufacturer
BYI	Baker-York Incorporated (Subsidiary of Otis Elevator Corporation)
CAD	Curtis Automotive Devices, Incorporated
CAE	Cresci Aviation Equipment Company
CAL	Colovar Corporation
CAS	Cargo Systems (Division of Koehring Company)
CAR	Carson Trailers
CER	Certified Stainless Service
CBC	Chain Belt Company
CDC	CONDEC Corporation
CDE	Consolidated Diesel Electric Corp.
CEC	Climax Engineering Company
CHC	Chrysler Corporation
CHM	Chemetron Corporation
CIM	Citation Manufacturing Company, Inc.
CLC	Century Electric Company
CLE	Clark Equipment Company
CMC	Cushman Motor Company
CMD	Chevrolet Motor Division
CME	Caterpillar Military Engine Company
CMI	C&M Industries Association, Inc.
CMW	Charles Machine Works, Inc.
CNM	Continental Motor Corp.
COL	Columbus Equipment Company
COM	Construction Machinery Company
COR	Corbitt Company
COS	Colson Corporation
CPT	Chicago Pneumatic Tool Company
CRP	Curtis Ryna Products Corp.
CSE	COPCO Steel and Engineering Company
CST	Columbian Steel Tank Company
CUM	Cummins, Incorporated
CTC	Caterpillar Tractor Company
DAC	DeVilbiss Air Compressor Company
DAI	Dahatsu, Inc.
DBG	Daybrook-Bowling Green
DBI	Dempster Brothers, Inc.
DCC	Davey Compressor Company
DDC	Dodge Division, Chrysler-Damlier Benz Corp.
DDS	Dempster-Dumpster Systems
DLC	Delco Products, Inc.
DMC	Davis Manufacturing Company

Table 8-3.--Manufacturer Codes--Continued.

Code	Manufacturer
DMG	Drott Manufacturing Company
DOU	Double A Trailers
DRD	Drexel Dynamic Corporation
DTI	Dorsey Trailer Corporation
DTM	Diamond T. Motor Company
DWO	D. W. Onan and Sons, Incorporated
DWT	Ditch Witch of North Carolina
DYN	Dynaweld
EAS	East Manufacturing Corp.
EBC	Eveready Brikson Company
ECC	E. C. Campbell, Incorporated
EDE	E. D. Etnyre and Company, Incorporated
EDI	Edison Incorporated
EEE	Elauar Manufacturing Company
ELD	Euclid
ELM	Electric Machinery Manufacturing Company
EMC	Essick Manufacturing Company
EMG	Empire Generator
EMI	Emico Corporation
EMP	Eaton Metal Products Company
ENM	Engler Manufacturing Company
ENW	Elliott Machine Works
EQS	Equipment Service Company
ESC	Elgin Sweeper Company
ETP	Eastern Tank of Peabody Incorporated
EXB	Excel Body Corporation
EXG	Ezgo Company
FAC	Face American of GA.
FAN	Fantuzzi U.S.A. Inc.
FAW	Federal Aircraft Works
FAY	Fayette Manufacturing
FCA	Farmers Chemical Association, Incorporated
FCC	Ford Machinery and Chemical Corporation
FCE	Fire Control Engineer Company
FEI	Fulgram Enterprise, Incorporated
FGH	Frank C. Hough Company
FHT	Freuhauf Trailer Company
FJC	Fitzjohn Coach Company
FMA	Fire Master Corporation
FMC	Farbanks Morse Company
FMD	Ford Motor Division
FME	Ferree Motors and Equipment Company

Table 8-3.--Manufacturer Codes--Continued.

Code	Manufacturer
FMF	FMC Corporation, John Bean Division
FPI	Fabricon Products, Incorporated
FRM	Farmount Railway Motors Incorporated
FTE	Fontaine Truck Equipment Company
FTI	Fire Trucks, Incorporated
GBC	Gilson Brothers Company
GCI	Gray Company, Incorporated
GDC	Good Motors Machine, Incorporated
GEC	General Electric Corporation
GHC	Gladhill Road Machine Company
GHT	G. H. Tennent Company
GIW	Gallion Iron Works and Manufacturer
GLC	Gerlinger Carrier Company
GLO	G. L. Cornell Company
GMC	General Motors Corporation
GNS	Greenville Steele Car Company
GMO	Grant mfg. Co.
GRA	Gradall, Inc.
GRO	Gorman-Rupp Company
GRM	Grove Manufacturing Company
GSC	General Safety Equipment Corporation
GTC	Gramm Trailer Corporation
GTO	Gravely Tractor Company
GVM	Giant Vacuum Manufacturing Company
GWC	Griffin Wellpoint Corporation
HAR	Harnischfeger Corporation
HBC	Huber Wasco Company
HBQ	Hobart Brothers Company
HCM	Hanson Clutch and Machine
HCR	Hesston Corporation
HDC	Harley Davidson Company
HDE	Hadco Engineering
HEC	Highway Equipment Company
HLC	Heil Company
HMC	Huber Manufacturing Company
HON	Honda Motor Company
HTC	Hamilton Trailer Company
HWC	Highway Trailer Company
HYC	Hyster Company
IED	Industrial Engine Department
IFM	International Fermont Machine Company

Table 8-3.--Manufacturer Codes--Continued.

Code	Manufacturer
IHC	International Harvester Corporation
IND	Indrustrious, Corp.
IRC	Ingerson Rand Company
ISO	Isometrics Incorporated
ISS	International Signal System
ISU	Isuzu Motor Company
ITM	ITT Marlon
JAC	Jackson, Inc.
JBD	John Bean Division
JCB	J.C. Bamford Corporation
JCC	J. Chase Corporation
JDA	J. D. Adams Manufacturing Company
JDC	John Deere
JDD	John Dean
JGM	Jaeger Machine Company
JIC	J. I. Case Company
JMC	Jacobsen Manufacturing Company
JON	Johnson, Corp.
JPI	Jeta Power Incorporated
KAL	Kalyn Incorp.
KAT	Kato Engineering Company
KEC	Kelite Corporation
KEH	Keith-Huber, Inc.
KHC	Kohler Company
KJC	Kaiser Jeep Corporation
KKC	Kut-Kwick Corporation
KMC	Kentucky Manufacturing Company
KOM	Kamatsu
KRC	Kur and Rout Company
KRG	Koehring Company
KWK	Kwik Mix Company
LAC	Louis Allis Company
LAW	Lawnel Corporation
LBC	Littleford Brothers Incorporated
LDI	Lodol Incorporated
LHR	Laher Manufacturing Company
LIC	Lilliston Implement Company
LIE	Lincoln Electric Company
LIT	Lift King, Inc.
LMC	Linding Manufacturing Company, Incorporated
LOR	Lorraine cranes

Table 8-3.--Manufacturer Codes--Continued.

Code	Manufacturer
LRC	LeRoi Company
LTC	LaCrosse Trailer Corporation
LWC	Libby Welding Company
MAC	U.S. Marine Corps 1/
MAH	Marlow Herrington
MAO	Myers Ashland, Ohio
MAT	Moble Aerial Towers, Incorporated
MAZ	Mazda Motor, Corp.
MBC	Meili-Blumburg Corporation
MCI	Mack Truck, Incorporated
MCT	Miley Circle M Trailer Company, Incorporated
MEC	Mercury Manufacturing Company
MEF	Miller Electric Manufacturing Company
MFC	Marden Manufacturing Company
MFI	Massey Ferguson, Incorporated
MHI	Mitsubishi
MID	Mid-Atlantic Trailers
MII	Motec Industries Incorporated
MKT	Markteer Company
MMC	Malsbary Manufacturing Company
MMD	Mercury Motor Car Division
MNN	Minneapolis Moline Company
MOT	Mott Corporation
MPC	Marlow Pump
MPR	Marion Power Shovel Company
MPS	Michigan Power Shovel Company
MRS	MRS Manufacturing Company
MSC	Miller Spreader
MTC	Motor Truck Company Cleveland
MTI	Miller Trailers, Incorporated
MWM	Maths Welding and Machine Company
MYB	F. F. Myers and Brothers
NAV	Navistar
NEC	Northwest Engineering Company
NIP	Nippon Yusoki
NI3	Nissan, Inc.
NMC	Northwestern Motor Company
NMO	National Mower Company
NWM	Northwest Motor Company

1/ Marine Corps tactical equipment transferred to the GME
   fleet.

Table 8-3.--Manufacturer Codes--Continued.

Code	Manufacturer
OBC	O'Brien Manufacturing Company
OCO	Olathe Manufacturing Company
OEC	Otis Elevator Company (Baker Division)
OHG	Ohio Galvanizing
OLC	Oliver Corporation
OMC	Olson Manufacturing Company
OML	Outboard Marine Corps - Lincoln
ONA	Onen
PDC	Plymouth Division, Chrysler Corporation
PER	Peerless Mfg.Co.
PGC	Pennington Manufacturing Company
PIC	Pierce mfg. Inc
PII	Progress Industries, Incorporated
PMC	Pettibone Mulliken Corporation
PMM	PAK-MOR Manufacturing Company
POL	Polaris Corp
PRM	Prime-Mover Company
PRT	Pro Tainer, Inc.
PSI	PSI Mobile Products, Incorporated
PSL	Mobile Products, Incorporated
PTC	Pettibone Corporation
PTD	Pullman Trail Mobile Division
PUI	Prismo Universal, Incorporated
QPC	Queensboro Packing Corporation
QTS	Quick-Way Truck Shovel Company
RAC	Raymond Corporation
RAY	Rayco, Inc.
RBC	Ralph B. Carter Company
RCC	Ross Carrier Corporation
REX	Rex Chainbelt Company
REY	Reynolds Company
RGL	R. G. Letuoreau, Incorporated
RIO	Reo Motors, Incorporated
RLE	Ryan Landscaping Equipment Company
RMC	Rogers Manufacturing Company, Incorporated
RMM	Roseman Mower Company
RNC	Ronning Corporation
ROB	Rogers Brothers Corporation
RPC	Rome Plow Company
RPE	Richmond Power Equipment Company, Incorporated
RSC	Roscoe Manufacturing Company

Table 8-3.--Manufacturer Codes--Continued.

Code	Manufacturer
RSS	Reach-All Sales and Service
SAG	Saginan Products Corporation
SAI	Soil Air Industries
SBC	Swab Wagon Company
SCH	Schwarze Ind.
SCM	Southern Coach Manufacturing Company
SEA	Seaman Motors
SEC	Session Equipment Company
SFC	Satuffer Trailer Company
SHC	Silent Hoist and Crane Company, Incorporated
SII	Schreck Industries, Incorporated
SIM	Simplicity Manufacturing Company
SIO	Sioux Steam Cleaner Corporation
SMC	Speciality Manufacturing Company
SMM	Schramm, Incorporated
SMS	Schramming
SMW	SCM Mower
SNI	Sanders Industries
SPC	Studebaker Packard Corporation
SSC	Stewart-Steele Corporation
SSL	Spenser-Stafford Loadcraft
SSS	Stewart and Stevenson System, Incorporated
STB	Stoughton, Truck Body, Incorporated
STC	Service Truck and Caster Corporation
STE	Stevens Manufacturing
STP	Step Manufacturing Company
STT	Sportcraft Travel Trailers
SUB	Suburu
SUL	Sullair Corporation
SWE	Sweinhart Electric Company
SWP	Sweeprite, Manufacturing
TBU	The Buda Company
TCO	Tennant Company
TCM	TCM of America
TDC	Taylor Dunn
TDD	Todd Combustion Equipment Company
TDS	Todd Shipyard Corporation
TEC	Trail-ET and Company
THC	Thickol Chemical Corporation
THD	The Hardie Manufacturing Corporation
THU	Theure, Incorporated
TIC	Tycodyne Industries Corporation

Table 8-3.--Manufacturer Codes--Continued.

Code	Manufacturer
TKC	Terrain King Corporation
TKM	Tractomotive Corporation
TMC	Tow Motor Corporation
TMI	T. M. Industries
TOR	Toro Manufacturing Company
TOY	Toyota Motor Corp.
TPC	Tankraft Products Corporation
TRA	Trailmobile, Inc.
TRC	Troyler Corporation
TRN	Trailnor, Corp.
TRP	Triumph Machinery Company
TTI	Transport Trailers, Incorporated
TUR	Turtle mfg. Co.
TWM	Towner Manufacturing Company
TYM	Tymco,Inc
UCR	Unit Crane and Shovel Corporation
UMC	Universal Motor Company
UNM	Unimasco Incorporated
USM	United States Motor Corporation
UTC	United Tractor Company
UTI	United Tractor, Incorporated
VER	Vermeer Manufacturing Company
VIC	Victor Manufacturing Company
VMC	Viking Manufacturing Company
UL	Vulcan Trailer Manufacturing Company
AB	Westinghouse Air Brake Company
WAI	Waldon, Incorporated
WAK	Walker Manufacturing Company
WAR	Wabco Equipment Company
WBC	West Bend Equipment Corporation
WCE	White Construction Corporation
WDP	Wolvering Diesel Power Company
WDR	Woolridge Manufacturing Company
WEB	Weber White Volovo, Inc
WEC	Westinghouse Electric Corporation
WEG	W. E. Grace Manufacturing Company
WEL	Wells Cargo, Inc.
WES	Westcoaster Company
WIS	Wisconsin Motor Corporation
WKC	Watter Kidded Company, Incorporated
WLC	Wiggins Lift Company

Table 8-3.--Manufacturer Codes--Continued.

Code	Manufacturer
WLD	Wald Industrial
WLF	Ward - LaFrance Truck Corporation
WMB	William Brothers Boiler Manufacturing Company
WMC	Worthington Mower Company
WMH	White Materials Handling Division
WOD	Woode Division Hesston Corporation
WOM	Willys-Overland Motors Corporation
WRS	Warner Swasey
WRT	Worthington Corporation
WSD	Weston Dump Body Company
WSP	West Point Products Company
WWW	Wendell and Sons
WYL	Wylie Manufacturing Company
WYN	Wayne Manufacturing Company
YNG	Young Sweeper Division - Sherry Saez
YTC	Yale Towne Corporation/Materials Handling
YZO	Yazoo Manufacturing Company, Incorporated

GARRISON MOBILE EQUIPMENT

CHAPTER 9

INSPECTION, TESTING, AND CERTIFICATION OF LOAD LIFTING
EQUIPMENT

9-1

GARRISON MOBILE EQUIPMENT

CHAPTER 9

INSPECTION, TESTING, AND CERTIFICATION OF LOAD LIFTING
EQUIPMENT

9000. BACKGROUND

1. This chapter provides standard procedures for the inspection,
testing, and certification of GME load lifting equipment. The
DoD requires all components, including the Marine Corps, to
conform to the Department of Labor's Occupational Safety and
Health Administration (OSHA) regulations (with some exceptions
predicated by defense missions). GME fleet managers will comply
with the applicable portions of 29 CFR 1910 and 29 CFR 1926,
taking particular note of the requirements contained in 29 CFR
1926.550, 551, and 602 and 29 CFR 1910.178 and 180, with regard
to the inspection, testing and certification of load lifting
equipment.

2. The procedures in this chapter apply to each unit owning or
using GME load lifting equipment. This includes all mobile load
lifting equipment commonly referred to as cranes, wreckers,
forklifts, and aerial personnel devices used to lift loads
vertically. Cranes, derricks, hoists, winches, and monorails,
which are permanently installed in facilities and are not mobile,
do not fall under the definition of GME and are not covered by
this Manual.

3. GME fleet managers will implement inspection, testing, and
certification programs per this Chapter.

9001. GENERAL INFORMATION

1. Table 9-1 lists requirements for inspection, testing, and
certification of GME load lifting equipment. GME fleet managers
will consult the manufacturer's technical publication to
determine the test load weight for each particular item tested.

2. Operators of load lifting GME will perform a daily inspection
of their assigned equipment. GME fleet managers may locally
produce a sample Equipment Operator's Daily Checklist contained
in table 9-2 for this purpose. They will file and retain this
form with the trip ticket.

3. When set forth in technical directives as a SM check,
operators and/or maintenance personnel will conduct condition
inspections at the same time as SM using the Condition Inspection
Record shown in table 9-3. If the SM services do not require a

general inspection, or where inspection requirements are not adequately covered, GME fleet managers will conduct condition inspections as set forth in this chapter.

4. GME fleet managers will conduct condition inspections prior to placing any load lifting equipment into service, whether newly fielded or received from another installation. Upon receipt of mobile cranes, aerial personnel devices, and forklifts used to lift ammunition, whether newly fielded or received from another installation, they will conduct load tests as part of the equipment acceptance inspection unless the item of equipment has valid certifications issued within the previous 12 months.

5. Only mobile cranes (including wreckers), forklifts used to lift ammunition, and aerial personnel devices require load testing. Aerial personnel devices include any mechanically, hydraulically, or electrically operated device used to lift a person in the air. Regularly scheduled periodic load testing is not required. GME fleet managers will conduct load tests on the following two occasions:

    a. Prior to the initial placement into service of mobile cranes, aerial personnel devices, and forklifts used to lift ammunition, whether newly fielded or received from another installation, if the equipment was received without a valid load test certificate issued within the previous 12 months 1/.

        1/ All contracts for the purchase of new mobile cranes or aerial personnel devices will include a requirement for a manufacturer's load test certification issued within the previous 12 months to accompany the vehicle on delivery.

    b. After extensive repairs (removal, replacement, or adjustment) to the lifting portion of cranes, forklifts used to lift ammunition, and aerial personnel devices. (For example, repairs to the truck portion of a mobile crane will not require load testing of the crane portion.) Outriggers are part of the lifting portion of cranes and aerial personnel devices.

6. GME fleet managers will use their supporting maintenance facilities to accomplish load testing activities, unless the manufacturer, repair contractor, or depot, as appropriate, provides written certification that testing has been conducted within the previous 12 months. Therefore, upon receipt of a mobile crane or aerial personnel device, the GME fleet manager will determine if a load test has been accomplished within the previous 12 months by examination of the equipment records. If no certification is present, the GME fleet manager may elect to

refuse to accept the equipment or arrange to have it locally load tested 2/.

> 2/ Contracts with repair contractors for rebuild
> or significantly repaired mobile cranes or aerial
> personnel devices will contain a load test
> requirement and certification clause. Depots
> will furnish the same.

7. Annual Condition Inspection. The purpose of the annual condition inspection is to ensure that the overall structural, mechanical, hydraulic, and electrical components of the equipment have been maintained in a safe and serviceable condition and function properly.

8. Certification. The certifying officer is responsible for ensuring the safety and reliability of all load lifting equipment. Installation commanders will appoint the certifying officer in writing. Certifying officers will either be Marine officers or qualified civilians 3/. The Marines will possess Military Occupational Specialty (MOS) 1310, 3510, or 2110. The certifying officer will, in turn, designate the authorized test directors and inspection and test personnel. Load test certifications will be based on the condition inspection and proof of load test certification. The test director, inspection and test personnel, and certifying officer will each sign the certification of condition inspection and/or load test.

> 3/ Certification officers should be qualified at an
> appropriate Marine Corps School or Labor Department
> approved civilian-run school.

9. Certification Frequency. GME fleet managers will certify the condition inspection of each item of load lifting equipment at least once annually.

10. Waivers. Units desiring waivers to load testing requirement will submit their requests to the CMC (LFS-2).

11. Marking. GME fleet managers will stencil load lifting equipment in a position clearly visible to the operator, with certification data indicating the test status.

> Example: CAP. 3,000 lbs. Certified 5 May 1999

9002. ANNUAL CONDITION INSPECTION. In addition to those inspections required by load lifting equipment TM's or commercial manuals, GME fleet managers will perform the following inspections (as applicable):

1. <u>All Load Lifting Equipment</u>

     a. Inspect all mechanical controls for proper adjustments
and inspect the entire control mechanism for excessive wear of
components and contamination by leaking lubricants or foreign
matter.

     b. Inspect hydraulic system seals, hoses, lines, fittings,
pumps, and valves, for deterioration, leaks, and wear.

     c. Inspect mast and lift carriage assemblies including forks
and chains, for cracks, broken welds, distortion, improper fit,
and excessive wear, rust, or corrosion.

     d. Inspect the brake and steering systems for excessively
worn or defective moving parts to include seat switches, parking
brakes, and brake interlock switches.

     e. Inspect electrical, gasoline, and diesel systems for
signs of malfunction, excessive deterioration, dirt or moisture
accumulation, and compliance with applicable safety regulations.

     f. Inspect protective motor control circuit devices, battery
cable connectors, battery compartment insulation, thermal
protectors, compartment covers, filters, and emergency switches
for proper installation, operation, and compliance with
applicable safety regulations.

     g. If required, correct and complete repairs of any
deficiencies prior to load testing.

2. <u>Hook Inspection</u>

     a. <u>General Inspection</u>. Inspect hooks annually for wear in
swivels and pins, other wear, cracks or gouges, and proper
operation and condition of safety latches, where installed.
Remove cracks and gouges parallel to the contour of the hook by
surface abrasion, resulting in a smooth surface retaining the
profile of the hook. When unable to remove cracks and gouges by
surface abrasion, discard the hook. Where cracks and gouges are
transverse to the contour of the hook, evaluate the hook for
retention or disposal. Defects in the unstressed portion of the
hook do not affect strength. Make no attempt to correct hook
deficiencies by use of heat or welding. Where normal wear or
removal of cracks or gouges results in a reduction in the
original sectional dimension of 10 percent or more, discard the
hook. Discard the hook if visually bent or twisted. Make no
attempt to straighten bent or twisted hooks.

b. <u>Hook Throat Spread</u>. Measure hooks for hook throat spread upon receipt. Establish a throat dimension base measurement by installing two tram points and measuring the distance between these tram points (to nearest 1/64th inch). See Figure 9-1. Retain this base dimension in the "remarks" section of the applicable equipment record jacket for the life of the hook. Measure the distance between tram points quarterly. Discard any hook showing an increase in the throat opening by more than 15 percent from the base measurement.

c. <u>Hook Disassembly, Inspection, and Nondestructive Test</u>. Annually inspect the hook, retaining nut, and bearings. Visually examine the hook and retaining nut for thread wear and corrosion damage. Visually inspect the block bearing plate for cracks, wear, or other damage. Inspect bearings for unusual wear and free rotation. Lubricate all components, as required, during re-assembly. Nondestructively test the entire hook and retaining nut assembly for structural defects. The nondestructive test of general-purpose crane hooks is valid for five certification periods. Use the crane certification date as the effective date of hook inspection and nondestructive test. Perform nondestructive tests as part of load tests (see paragraph 9003.3b(3)(a)2).

3. <u>Inspection of Wire Rope, Fastenings, and Terminal Hardware</u>

a. <u>General Procedures</u>. Remove the wire rope dressing from those areas exposed to maximum wear, exposure, and abuse. Inspect for crushing, kinks, corrosion, broken wires, and proper lubrication. Check the wire rope sockets, swage fittings, eye swivels, trunnions, stays, pendants, and securing hardware for wear, cracks, corrosion, and other damage. Disconnect or disassemble the drum end fittings only when visible evidence of deterioration deems it necessary.

b. <u>Wire Rope Rejection Criteria</u>. Remove the damaged portions, or replace all wire rope exceeding the following:

(1) <u>Kinks or Crushed Sections</u>. Severe kinks or crushed rope in straight runs where the core is forced through the outer stands or wires are damaged. (This does not apply to runs around eyes, thimbles, and shackles.)

(2) <u>Flattened Sections</u>. Flattened sections where the diameter across the flat is less than five-sixth of original diameter. (This does not apply to runs around eyes, thimbles, and shackles.)

(3) Wear. Not to exceed 30 percent of any individual outer wire diameter.

(4) Broken Wires

(a) Running Ropes. The number of broken or torn wires exceeds six randomly distributed broken or torn wires in one lay or three broken wires in one strand in one lay. Replace the end connection if there is one or more broken wires adjacent to the end connection.

(b) Standing, Guy, and Boom Pendant Ropes. More than two broken wires in one lay in sections beyond the end connection or one or more broken wires at an end connection.

(5) Loss in Diameter. Not to exceed 10 percent of the nominal diameter of the wire rope.

(6) Accumulation of Defects. An accumulation of defects which in the judgment of the inspector creates an unsafe condition.

(7) Rated Capacity. The rated capacity of replacement wire rope for all cranes will be per the manufacturer's stated requirements. Maintain a certification of the breaking strength of all replacement rope in the equipment maintenance record.

(8) Wire ropes shall be removed from service and replaced if there is any evidence of heat damage from any cause.

4. Hoists, Winches, and Structural Metal Components

a. Operation Check. The operator will perform an operation check as prescribed in the appropriate technical manuals. For equipment that does not have a checklist included in the technical manual, operators will conduct the following inspection as a minimum requirement:

(1) Inspect all control mechanisms for proper adjustment and operation.

(2) Inspect all control mechanisms for any excessive wear of components and contamination by lubricants or other foreign matter.

(3) Inspect all safety and locking devices for proper function.

b. Condition Inspection. Before, during, and after each annual test or calibration, inspect for the following, as applicable:

(1) General Information

    (a) Check for proper marking.

    (b) Check for evidence of mishandling and/or damage.

    (c) Check for excessive wear on brake and clutch system linings, pawls, and ratchets.

    (d) Check rope reeving for compliance with manufacturer's specifications.

    (2) Frames. Check for bends, distorted sections, broken welds, excessive corrosion, and loose bolts or rivets.

5. Recording of Annual Condition Inspection. GME fleet managers will use the form contained in table 9-3 to record (as applicable) the Annual Condition Inspection of Load Lifting Equipment. Record and certify required load tests as shown in the sample form contained in table 9-4. This form may be locally printed.

9003. LOAD TESTING. The following paragraphs apply when cranes or aerial personnel devices require local load testing:

1. Facilities. Load testing mobile cranes and aerial personnel devices require the following facilities:

    a. A sufficiently large, level hard stand.

    b. A dead-man strong enough to withstand at least 150 percent of the area's largest mobile crane's capacity.

    c. A calibrated Baldwin SR-4 load cell, or its equivalent, with a capacity of measuring at least 150 percent of the area's largest mobile crane's capacity.

    d. Calibrated weights heavy and dense (compact) enough for use in the load tests described.

2. Location of Facilities. Installation commanders of the following installations will provide facilities for the load testing of both GME and tactical equipment for all Marine Corps units in their geographical vicinity:

    a. MCCDC Quantico, Virginia

    b. MCB Camp Lejeune, North Carolina

    c. MCAS Beaufort, South Carolina

    d. MCB Camp Pendleton, California

    e. MCAS Cherry Point, North Carolina

    f. MCAS Miramar, California

    g. MCLB Albany, Georgia

    h. MCLB Barstow, California

    i. MCAS Kaneohe Bay, Hawaii

    j. MCB Camp Butler, Japan

    k. MCAS Iwakuni, Japan

3. <u>Load Tests</u>

    a. <u>General</u>

       (1) Prescribed tests are overload tests, and personnel conducting load tests should exercise extreme caution at all times. When testing lattice boom cranes, personnel will watch the outrigger(s) opposite the boom for any indication of the outrigger(s) leaving the ground. This condition indicates that the lifting device is approaching a tip-over condition. Immediately terminate the test by lowering the test load to the ground. When testing hydraulic boom cranes, an outrigger opposite a load positioned at a swing angle of 45, 135, 225, and 315 degrees (measured from the front of the vehicle as 0 degrees) may rise off the ground. This is not tipping. At no time during testing should two outriggers of a hydraulic boom crane rise off the ground. If this condition occurs, testing should immediately terminate by lowering the test load to the ground. Conduct a condition inspection per the instructions contained in paragraph 9002, preceding, prior to load testing.

       (2) Personnel will remain clear of suspended loads and areas where they could be struck in the event of boom failure.

       (3) Raise the test load only to a height sufficient to perform the test.

       (4) Do not use items of Marine Corps equipment as load testing weights.

       (5) Testing officials should consider the use of safety chains attached to outriggers on the side opposite the lift to preclude accidental rollover during maximum (overload) testing.

(6) Testing officials should consider the use of wooden cribbing under the crane's counterweight to prevent rear rollover in the event a wire rope or hook fails during maximum (overload) testing.

    b. <u>Cranes</u>

      (1) For truck cranes, extend outriggers and raise the crane carrier off the ground to completely unload tires or wheels. Level the crane as required by the manufacturer's load chart. Rotate the boom 90 degrees from the longitudinal axis of the crane carrier, and position the boom to the minimum-working radius.

      (2) <u>No-Load Tests</u>

        (a) <u>Hoist</u>

        <u>1</u> Raise and lower the hook through the full working distance of hook travel.

        <u>2</u> Run the hoist block into the limit switch(es), where installed, at slow speed.

        <u>3</u> Run the hoist block beyond the limit switch(es), where installed, by using the bypass switch.

        (b) <u>Boom</u>

        <u>1</u> Raise and lower the boom through the full working range.

        <u>2</u> Raise the boom into the upper limit switch, where installed. Raise the boom past the boom upper limit switch, using the bypass switch.

        <u>3</u> Test the lower limit switch, where installed, using the same procedure prescribed for testing the upper limit switch.

        <u>4</u> Extend and retract the telescoping boom sections through the full distance of travel.

        <u>5</u> Check the radius indicator by measuring the radius at the minimum and maximum boom angles.

        <u>6</u> Operate other motions, including swing, through one cycle (one full revolution of major components).

(3) Load Test. The load test consists of two parts: a maximum load test and a stability test. Perform the tests in the following described sequence:

(a) Maximum Test

_1_ With the position of the boom 90 degrees to the right or left of the lower carrier frame, raise the boom to the maximum prescribed lift angle. Attach the hook to the load lifting measuring device and verify the wire rope connecting the hook to the boom is in a vertical configuration (check wire rope with carpenter's level or plumb line). Ensure outriggers are at full horizontal extension with vertical jacks lowered to level the turntable bearing. Verify level turntable by placing a carpenter's level in direction of boom and 90 degrees to direction of boom. Ensure tires are off the ground during the test.

_2_ Lift the manufacturer's stated load test weight and hold for one minute. Slowly decrease load until wire rope is barely slack. Repeat this procedure once again. If the manufacture has no stated load test weight, use 110 percent of the crane's rated capacity. Following the two lifts, inspect hook as in paragraph 9002.2b, preceding. This hook inspection will serve as the nondestructive hook test.

(b) Stability Test

_1_ Choose any load from the load chart not in the black (shaded) structural strength area of the rated load 360 degrees chart. Chosen test load must clear outriggers during full 360-degree rotation.

_2_ Position the boom 90 degrees to either the right or left side of the lower carrier frame.

_3_ Place outriggers at full horizontal extension and lower vertical jacks to level the turntable bearing. Verify level turntable by placing a carpenter's level in direction of boom and 90 degrees to direction of boom. Ensure tires are off the ground during the test.

_4_ Position the hook block in a manner to obtain the appropriate operating test radius for tested boom length. Confirm by actual measurement, the operating radius to center of rotation. Adjust as necessary to obtain the specified radius.

_5_ Mark the tested radius with an arc about the axis of rotation using a line of sufficient width to ensure its visibility when the load traverses over it.

_6_ Position the test load inside the selected operating radius. The "Rated Load" is equal to the test weight plus hook block weight plus sling weights. Hook block and sling weights may vary by type used.

_7_ Boom up 2 to 4 degrees to position the hook block over the load and to compensate for boom deflection. Lift the rated load. Boom down while keeping load close to ground until the hook block is centered over the selected operating radius and suspends the rated load 2 to 4 inches above the ground.

_8_ Swing the crane through the 360 degrees rotation.

v Lower load.

c. Aerial Personnel Devices

(1) General Information. The sequence of inspection is: condition inspection, no-load test, and load test.

(2) Pre-operation. The operator will perform a pre-operation check as prescribed in the appropriate TM's. For equipment that does not have a checklist included in the manual, conduct the following as a minimum requirement:

(a) Position the vehicle on the test site.

(b) Check for proper markings.

(c) Carefully inspect all safety devices, including all specialized features.

(3) Condition Inspection. Conduct this inspection per the instructions contained in paragraph 9002, preceding.

(4) Load Test (Stability and Range of Movement). Conduct the load test with the vehicle not fastened to any artificial base, and with outriggers in place. Conduct all tests using the ground level controls. At no time will personnel ride on the platform (basket). Load the platform with an evenly distributed load equal to the manufacturer's standard test load and exercise through the full range of horizontal and vertical positions, to include at least the following:

(a) Move the upper and lower arms to a horizontal, or their most horizontal plane, and extend to the maximum reach.

(b) Move the lower arm to a horizontal, or near horizontal, position over the side of the vehicle, and the upper arm to the most vertical position possible.

(c) With the lower arm at the maximum travel from the towed position and the upper arm both horizontal and 45 degrees to the side of the vehicle, or over the four corners of the vehicle, rotate the turntable both clockwise and counter clockwise with the test load through 360 degrees for a minimum of 15 minutes.

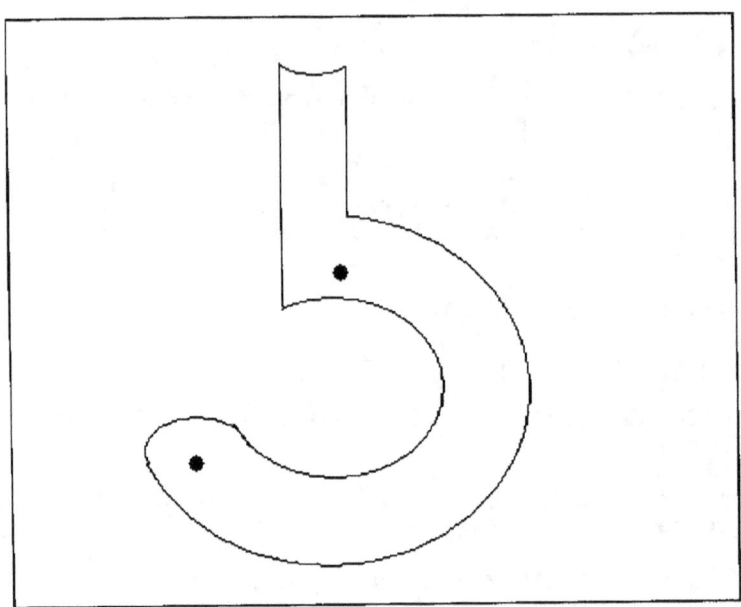

Figure 9-1.--Tram Points.

Table 9-1.--Inspection, Testing, and Certification
Requirements by Equipment Type.

	Forklifts	Wreckers and Retrievers	Mobile Cranes	Aerial Personnel Device
Validate Inspection Certificates Prior to Placing into Service	X	X	X	X
Annual Condition Inspection	X	X	X	X
Annual Hook Inspect		X	X	
Post-Maintenance No-Load Test	1/	X	X	X
Post-Maintenance Load Test	1/	X	X	X
Load Test Certification	1/	X	X	X
Stability & Range of Movement			X	X
Daily Ops Check	X	X	X	X

1/ Required only for forklifts used to lift ammunition.

9-15

GARRISON MOBILE EQUIPMENT

Table 9-2.--Operator's Daily Checklist.

USMC No.	Type/Cap	Location/Assignment	SHIFT 1 2 3	HOUR METER START STOP	HOURS Operated	DATE

Operator's Name	Oiler's Name	INSTRUCTIONS- Check all items indicated, inspect and indicate as satisfactory (S), unsatisfactory (U), or not applicable (NA).

1 WALK AROUND INSPECTION		S	U	2 MACHINERY HOUSE INSPECTION		S	U	3 OPERATOR CAB INSPECTION		S	U	4 OPERATION INSPECTION		S	U
a Safety Guards&Plates				a Housekeeping				a Gauges				a Area Safety			
b Carrier Frame/rotate base	*			b Engine/Compressor				b Warning/Indicator Lights				b Unusual Noises			
c General Hardware				c Leaks, Fuel/lube/oil/water				c Controls/Brakes				c Control Action			
d Wire Rope	*			d Lubrication				d Visibility				d Brakes/boom/load			
e Reeving	*			e Battery				e Load Rating Charts				e Crane Stability			
f Block	*			f Lights				f Safety Devices				f No Load Test			
g Hook	*			g Glass				g Emergency Stops				g Fleeting sheave			
h Sheaves	*			h Clutch/Brake Linings				h List/Trim indicators				h Limit Switches			
i Boom/Jib				i Electric Motors				i Boom Angle/radius indicator							
j Gantry/Pendants/boomstop	*			j Warning Tags											
K Walks/ladders/handrails				k Fire Extinguisher(s)											
l Windlocks/chocks/stops															
m Tires/wheels/tracks															
n Leaks, fuel/lube/oil/water															
o Radius indicator															
p Outrigger/locking Device	*														

INSTRUCTIONS- Inspect all applicable items indicated each shift. Suspend all operations immediately when observing an unsatisfactory condition of any item indicated above with an asterisk, thus (*). In addition, suspend operation if any unsafe condition is observed and immediately notify supervisor. Other conditions not affecting safety shall be noted under "Remarks" and reported to supervisor

OPERATOR'S SIGNATURE

DATE

REMARKS

Supervisor's SIGNATURE

CRANE OPERATOR'S DAILY CHECKLIST

DATE

AUTHORIZED FOR LOCAL REPRODUCTION

Table 9-3.---Condition Inspection Record.

USMC No: Type: Location: Operator Names: Optr License No.: Date of Inspection:				
Item No.	Item Description	P	F	Inspector's Initials
1	Bent, cracked, or corroded structural members.			
2	Cracked or corroded welds.			
3	Loose, broken, missing, or deteriorated rivets or bolts.			
4	Inspect all wire ropes for wear, broken wires, corrosion, kinks, damaged strands, crushed or flattened sections, condition of sockets, and Dead-end connections. Check for proper lubrication and evidence of proper inspection of idler sheaves and saddles.			
5	Inspect hooks for cracks, sharp edges, and distortion. Verify disassembly, inspection, and NDT, as applicable.			
6	Inspect all brakes and clutches for proper operation. Spot-check components for proper adjustment and acceptable wear.			
7	Check all controls for proper condition and operation.			
8	Check all control components for proper condition and operation.			

Table 9-3.--Condition Inspection Record--Continued.

Item No.	Item Description	P	F	Inspector's Initials
9	Inspect all limit switches for condition and proper operation.			
10	Ensure each drum has minimum of two complete wraps of wire rope at lowest working level.			
11	Check load indicators for condition and working accuracy.			
12	Inspect all mechanical equipment that is reasonably accessible for wear, cracks, and alignment.			
13	Inspect, where practical, for worn, defective, or misaligned bearings, bushings, shafts, pins, and gears.			
14	Check components for excessive heat, vibration, noises, and oil leaks.			
15	Inspect sheaves for wear, roughness, free turning, and alignment. Gauge sheave groove, where possible.			
16	Inspect for excessive wear of wheels, tires, rollers, and roller paths or rails.			
17	Inspect for excessive wear of chains and sprockets. Measure chain stretch of load chains.			
18	Verify that correct certified capacity charts or hook load rating data is in view of operator and/or rigging personnel.			

GARRISON MOBILE EQUIPMENT

Table 9-3.--Condition Inspection Record--Continued.

Item No.	Item Description	P	F	Inspector's Initials
19	Inspect operator's cab for cleanliness and operation of all equipment.			
20	Check machinery house for cleanliness, proper safety guards, warning signs, and storage of tools and equipment.			
21	Check operation of all indicators, warning devices, and lights.			
22	Check for proper type and condition of all fire protection equipment.			
23	Check condition and function of outriggers, pads, boxes, wedges, and cylinder mountings. Check level indicators.			
24	Check center pin nut and steadiment by observing operational behavior during load test.			
25	Check travel, steering, braking, and locking devices for condition and proper operation.			
26	Check radius indicator for accuracy by measuring actual radius in at least two boom positions.			
27	Check pawls, ratchets, and spuds for proper engagement and operation of interlocks.			
28	Inspect tanks, lines, valves, drains, filters, and other components of air systems for leakage and proper operation.			

Table 9-3.--Condition Inspection Record--Continued.

Item No.	Item Description	P	F	Inspector's Initials
29	Inspect reservoirs, pumps, motors, valves, lines, cylinders, and other components of hydraulic systems for leakage and proper operation.			
30	Check engines and engine generator sets for proper performance, safety, and system leakage.			
31	Inspect for bent, cracked, corroded, or dented boom members.			
32	Check condition of counterweights, ballast, and securing fasteners.			
33	Check all compartments (voids) for water tightness.			
34	Check accuracy of list and trim indicators against design data or previous test data.			

Remarks:

Signatures: Dates:

1. Inspector
_____

2. Test Director
_____

3. Certifying Officer
_____

Table 9-4.--Certification of Load Test.

USMC No.	Type	Rated Cap lbs._____ feet_____	Boom Length	Test Site		Test Date

Reason for test | **Certification**
This is to certify that inspections and tests have been conducted per the crane test procedures set forth in MCO P11262.2 and P11240.106.

Category Group (1) Cranes

Hoist	Test Load %	Minimum Radius Pounds Feet	Maximum Radius Pounds Feet
Main			
Aux			
Whip			

Crane Test Procedures Paragraph Numbers

Hook Throat Opening	Before Test	After Test
Main Hook		
Aux Hook		
Whip Hook		

Note 1. Enter the number of each paragraph complied with in MCO P11262.2 or MCO P11240.106. The former order applies to tactical equipment while the latter only to GME.

Crane Condition: Inspection Record item Numbers Check (✓) items inspected

1____	6____	11____	16____	21____	26____	31____	36____
2____	7____	12____	17____	22____	27____	32____	37____
3____	8____	13____	18____	23____	28____	33____	38____
4____	9____	14____	19____	24____	29____	34____	39____
5____	10____	15____	20____	25____	30____	35____	40____

It is further certified that the crane identified above is satisfactory to lift its rated capacity at its rated radii.

Test Director (Signature)	Date
Inspector (Signature)	Date
Certifying Official (Signature)	Date

www.ingramcontent.com/pod-product-compliance
Lightning Source LLC
Chambersburg PA
CBHW082243310526
45795CB00013B/2014